Opening and Operating A Bed & Breakfast In the 21st Century

Your Step-by-Step Guide to Innkeeping Success with Professional Online Marketing Strategies

By
Amelia Painter

Iowa Bed & Breakfast Innkeepers Association
Second Edition
November 2007

PO Box 171
Spencer, IA 51301
1-800-888-4667 (Iowa only) or 1-712-580-4242 (Outside Iowa)
www.iabedandbreakfast.com
E-mail: inns@iabedandbreakfast.com

ISBN: 1-4196-6057-8

Editors: Leslie Schultz, Marilyn Meyer, Katrina Anne Foley
Cover Design by Emily G. Boetel
Front Cover Photos by Amelia and Doug Painter were taken at the Log House & Homestead on Spirit Lake in Vergas, MN ~ www.loghousebb.com
Technical Advisor: Angie Roberts of Graphic Details ~ www.gdetails.com

This essential handbook for innkeepers is available for bulk purchase to associations, and for premium use by industry professionals. For details write or call the Iowa Bed & Breakfast Innkeepers Association at 1-800-888-4667 (Iowa only) or 712-580-4242 if you are calling from outside Iowa. You can also inquiry by mail at: IBBIA, PO Box 171, Spencer, IA 51301.

Printed and bound in the United States of America.
10 9 8 7 6 5 4 3 2

Notes:

Acknowledgments

I wish to thank the members of the Iowa Bed & Breakfast Innkeepers Association who voluntarily contributed innkeeping hints and tips for this guidebook.

This outstanding group is an independent organization of Iowa innkeepers dedicated to the promotion of quality bed and breakfasts. All members are regularly reviewed/inspected. This organization was the first in the nation to create an online inn traveler's blog, they constantly strive to provide new ideas to their members to enhance the bed and breakfast experience for their guests.

Gratitude is extended to my Technical Advisor, Angie Roberts, owner of Graphic Details, a design firm specializing in graphic design and print media. TotalWebDesigner.com is strategically partnered with Graphic Details to serve the Bed and Breakfast Innkeepers of America. Visit their Web site at www.gdetails.com for full information on their graphic design services for advertising, branding, logos, brochures and more. Angie specializes in small to medium size business relationships offering unsurpassed service with award winning design. Clients range from "Mom & Pop" businesses to Universal Studios, and everything in between.

Special appreciation is also extended to Emily G. Boetel for her support and graphic artistry. Emily's custom Web designs can be seen on bed and breakfast Web sites across the country. To learn more about Emily's work visit www.TotalWebDesigner.com.

Introduction

Bed and Breakfast (B&B) operations began early in America's history when homeowners began hosting travelers in boarding house settings. These operations thrived until changing travel trends and traveler demographics encouraged the development of large, modern hotels and motels which replaced many of the small B&B or boarding house businesses. While many innkeepers prefer the bed and breakfast type of operation, in the Midwest there remains a good number of boarding house businesses that combine boarding house and B&B offerings.

A desire for a unique lodging experience in small town America and the desire to seek out lodging in comfortable, homey environments have prompted a resurgence of the Bed and Breakfast Industry. B&Bs offer the traveler home-like hospitality that usually includes outstanding breakfast menus to start the day. Both business and pleasure travelers have re-discovered this lodging option.

Owning and operating a B&B can provide both financial and personal rewards for some individuals and families. This book provides information and guidelines for people who are considering joining the growing number of Americans who own and operate bed and breakfast establishments.

This book is not intended to serve as a source of city, county or state planning and health regulations because they vary from region to region and state to state. It is highly recommended that you contact the appropriate regulatory authorities in your specific area, early in your planning phase. Those authorities may include a county or city's planning department, finance department, community development director, mayor, building inspector, zoning administrator, town manager, town engineer, city health officials, county health department, or county administrator. Identify the appropriate regulatory authority in your area by talking to current B&B and small hotel owners.

Additional assistance is available both to new and existing bed and breakfast owners and those considering becoming owners. One excellent source is Amelia Painter and her creative team at www.TotalWebDesigner.com. They can be reached by phone at (712) 260-5372. Another excellent resource is your state bed and breakfast association.

If you are planning to open your establishment in Iowa, you'll want to join the Iowa Bed & Breakfast Innkeepers Association as an Aspiring Innkeeper early on and make an effort to attend some of their new innkeeper workshops and seminars. This is one of the country's leading state associations and they have an excellent Aspiring Innkeepers program. As a matter of fact, this book is given out to every IBBIA Aspiring Member and used as a textbook at their Aspiring Innkeepers Boot Camp Sessions.

Once you have opened the doors to your new bed and breakfast operation, you are eligible to join as a Full Member and request a mentor be assigned to guide you through your first year(s) of operation.

Contact their business office at 1-800-888-4667 (Iowa only) or 712-580-4242 (out-of-state callers) or you can visit the organization online at: www.iabedandbreakfast.com. You can also write to them at:

Iowa Bed & Breakfast Innkeepers Association

PO Box 171

Spencer, IA 51301

Notes:

Table of Contents

Notes:

Chapter One

Are You Sure You'd Make a Great Innkeeper?

If you've found yourself daydreaming about the independence and romance of owning your own bed and breakfast inn, then it's time to ask yourself some very serious questions. Every bed and breakfast and every B&B innkeeper is individual and unique, and it is these very qualities that can make for a successful operation. But, these same qualities can also be the downfall of a potentially successful operation. You, and only you, can answer the questions below. Be honest with yourself about the answers as they will affect the outcome of your life for the next few years.

Are you opening a B&B as primary source of income or as a hobby in your retirement years? Be clear on this answer as it will affect how you answer all the other questions that follow.

- Are you good with people? Are you flexible, patient, diplomatic, compassionate, well-organized, ambitious, and energetic?
- Have you fully evaluated your feelings about hospitality and serving guests?

- Will your B&B only be open during a specific season of the year? Or, year round?
- Do you know exactly how many hours a week you plan to work at the B&B?
- Have you written a list of your skills? (Accounting, housekeeping, cooking, cleaning, landscaping, marketing, using computers & other technology, maintenance, etc.)
- Have you completed a detailed business plan?
- Have you investigated the B&B Industry and made a commitment to it?

And, last but not least, have you given serious thought to how you feel about being tied down as you work nights, weekends and holidays?

All successful bed and breakfasts have one thing in common: owners who like people! Anyone seriously thinking about opening a bed and breakfast must like people and be able to deal with all types of people. This is a people business! You must also be willing to sacrifice a big part of your personal life since guests will be living with you.

How Well Do You Know Yourself?

Before spending a lot of time and money, use this personal assessment survey to help determine if you and your partner (if applicable) have the skills needed.

Answer the questions below, and again, it is critical that you be honest with yourself. Have your partner do the same.

Personal Assessment Survey

- I enjoy getting up early and preparing meals.
- I'm self-motivated and a self-starter.
- I'm highly organized and manage my time well.
- I enjoy serving people and entertaining.
- I'm tolerant and patient. I get along with most everyone. I can handle conflict well and remain calm under pressure.
- I can work long hours and adjust easily to a variety of interruptions.
- I am handy with tools and enjoy performing home maintenance.
- I'm cheerful and enjoy interior decorating.
- I love and enjoy gardening and landscaping.
- I'm financially stable and have another source of regular income.

- I'm a good communicator: on the phone, in-person and in-writing.
- I'm persistent and tenacious. I don't give up easily.
- I have a high energy level.
- I consider myself flexible and can easily handle emergencies.
- I have a good business sense.
- I can handle the accounting/business end of a bed and breakfast operation.

What are your strengths and weaknesses? Do your strengths outweigh your weaknesses? If not, how will you deal with the weaknesses you've identified? (If you have a partner, be sure you compare your answers so you can identify the combined weaknesses that must be planned for.)

Running a bed and breakfast is real work. Your guests expect clean rooms, delicious breakfasts, and service that goes way above and beyond that of the local hotel or motel. You'll need to get up early, often get to bed late and -- at least in the beginning -- you'll have to do the majority (if not all) of the cleaning. You'll be meal planning, shopping for groceries and supplies, doing the meal prep work that often seems never ending and preparing the meals for guests while you are managing the business on a daily basis. And, I do mean managing. Records must be kept, forms filled out, and daily bookkeeping tasks cannot be overlooked. Keeping good records increases a new business' chances of survival and an established business' chances of staying in business and earning good profits. Are you up to the challenge?

One of the best personality sorters out there is the *The Keirsey Temperament Sorter*. It is a 70-question personality instrument that helps individuals identify their personality type. The sorter is based on Dr. David Keirsey's Temperament theory and has helped over 30 million people worldwide to gain insight into themselves and the people around them. This insight is useful when selecting a career or choosing a work environment. Learn more online at: http://www.keirsey.com. (Jerry Phillips, affectionately referred to by many innkeepers as the "Father of Bed & Breakfast," highly recommends using this tool to learn more about yourself and, most importantly, if you are well-suited for a career as an innkeeper.)

Prior to purchasing an existing bed and breakfast operation, I worked at a successful inn for over a year. This apprentice experience gave me the hands-on insights and training I needed prior to investing my own money in an existing business. It also gave the opportunity to make sure my personality would be suited for my chosen career path. I realize this is not an option that every aspiring innkeeper can take advantage of, but I believe its one that should be seriously considered by all aspiring innkeepers.

I also want to encourage anyone considering the purchase of an existing bed and breakfast to be sure they request all the accounting data from the past three years and review it with a banker, CPA or accountant prior to submitting an offer to purchase the property.

Pamela K. Adams
Metcalf House
226 Geneseo
Storm Lake, IA 50588
www.metcalfhouse.com

Ready to Purchase a Property or Turn Your Current Homestead into a B&B?

Be Sure You Can Answer These 29 Questions!

Every bed and breakfast and every innkeeper is individual and unique. You, and only you can answer the questions below. Be honest about the answers as it is your life and your future that will be affected.

1. Think you have found the property of your dreams? Have you checked into the zoning of it locally? Is the property zoned for your type of B&B operation? Are there any building code constraints you must consider?
2. Have you purchased the property contingent upon gaining approval for a B&B from the local authorities? (Your City, Town or County?)
3. If you are purchasing an existing B&B, have you and your accountant, attorney or banker reviewed financial records & tax returns for the last 3 years of operation?
4. Will you be able to obtain specific B&B insurance – not just a rider to a homeowners' policy? (Most state bed and breakfast associations require members to carry a commercial insurance policy geared to the hospitality industry. Not all properties are eligible for this specialized type of coverage.)
5. What are the strengths and weaknesses of the location?
6. What is the potential for future growth and expansion?
7. Are the immediate neighbors in favor of your proposed operation?
8. Are the local economic and lodging trends favorable to your operation?
9. Do you know the trends occurring in the B&B industry?

10. Do you really know your competition?
11. Do you know the type of B&B guest that will be attracted to this location? Can you describe your target audience? (Age, income level, interests, etc.)
12. Do you know the occupancy levels and average room rates you could ultimately achieve at this location? As any savvy real estate salesperson will tell you, it's all about location, location, location!
13. Do you know exactly how many hours a week you plan to work at the B&B? Do you or your spouse have a full-time job that will sustain you when occupancy is down?
14. Have you completed a detailed business plan?
15. Will your B&B only be open during a specific season of the year? Or, year round?
16. Will your primary business come during the week or only on week-ends?
17. Are you opening a B&B as a for-profit business or as a hobby in your retirement years?
18. Do you know your state's "sales tax" licensing requirements?
19. Have you investigated the Heath Department regulations for your area?
20. Will you computerize your bookkeeping system? If yes, will you need to take classes? If so, have you looked into local classes as well as online resources for the training? (www.ed2o.com has excellent online courses.)
21. What type of a reservation program will you institute?
22. Have you investigated accepting real-time reservations on the Internet?
23. Have you investigated the B&B Industry and made a commitment to it?
24. Have you fully evaluated your feelings about hospitality and serving guests?

25. Have you written a list of yours and your partners' skills? (Financial, housekeeping, cooking, cleaning, computer, marketing, maintenance, etc.) If neither of you have computer skills, will you be able to take classes near-by?
26. Do you know which tasks and services you'll hire a professional to attend to?
27. Are you good with people? Are you flexible, patient, diplomatic, organized, ambitious and energetic?
28. Have you started writing your policies and guidelines regarding children, pets, smoking, cancellations, minimum stays, type of breakfast, accepting credit cards, and the times of day you desire guests to check-in and check-out?
29. Do you have a name for your inn?
    a. Designed a logo?
    b. Created a slogan?
    c. Selected your marketing color palette?
    d. Designed your business card and stationery?
    e. Designed your rack card or brochure?

And, last but not least, have you given serious thought to how you feel about being tied down as you work nights, week-ends and holidays? Or how your spouse and/or family members feel about living in an environment that makes demands on their time, energy and resources?

While there are a great many rewards connected to owning and operating a bed and breakfast establishment, you must seriously and honestly address all the potential damage that could be brought upon a marriage or a family unit that is not as thrilled as you are about the idea of having strangers come into your home for overnight, week-end, and sometimes, weekly stays.

Sit down with all family members and discuss the following questions and their answers:

- Does every member of the family enjoy meeting, talking, and interacting with people?

- Is the family comfortable with the idea of having and serving strangers in the home?

- Is the family comfortable with all types of people from different cultures and socioeconomic backgrounds?

- Will every family member be open to giving up their privacy?

- Will every family member enjoy keeping the property neat and clean as well as cook and serve strangers?

If, after a prolonged discussion, the answers to these questions are all on the positive side, it is possible that you and your family might prove to be successful B&B owners-operators. If the responses weigh heavier on the negative side, you should reconsider the idea of opening a B&B.

My best suggestion to aspiring innkeepers is to seek out a state bed & breakfast organization. It is tough to go it all alone. I did check out and hook up with the Iowa Bed & Breakfast Innkeepers Association (IBBIA) pretty quickly when I started out, and I know they got me through some tough times. Get a mentor -- some one else who is, or has been, a successful innkeeper who is willing to share with you and to listen to you. Visit lots of inns, ask questions, questions, questions, and read innkeeping publications like this one. If you love to take care of guests, share with others and help people have a fun relaxing time in your home, this may be the right industry for you. Check it out by attending a state bed & breakfast conference in your area. You just might get hooked for life. I know I did!

Esther Kauffeld-Hoffa
Garden and Galley B&B
1321 S. Jefferson Way
Indianola, IA 50125
www.gardenandgalley.com

What is it Going to Cost to Open the Doors?

The initial cost of opening a bed and breakfast establishment varies. If you already own the property the cost will be less than if you must go out and purchase. If you buy an existing B&B, many of your expenses could be lower if plan to just step-in and take over "as is." But, one thing is generally true, no matter what your situation, most new innkeepers usually spend a lot more than they first anticipate, that is why it is so important to actually put a pencil and paper to it --- so you will have an accurate picture of the amount of money you will need to get started. If you have no property acquisition costs involved, the costs to consider may include the following:

- renovations (electrical, plumbing, kitchen updates, replacing windows, landscaping, fixtures, roof work, security system, etc.)
- interior decoration (painting, replacing furniture, wallpapering, updating lighting, etc.)
- linens (bedding, kitchen and table)
- Towels
- Dishes, kitchenware and utensils
- smoke and carbon monoxide detectors, fire extinguishers, and other emergency equipment
- Signage (interior and exterior)

- Promotional and advertising materials (brochures, rack cards, Web site, ads, etc.)
- permits and licenses (local and state registrations, privilege or business license, and food service permit or license)
- insurance (liability, medical, property, vehicle, workers comp, etc.)
- computer, printer, fax, copier, telephone with answering service/machine, Wifi service
- office software and supplies (computer software, stationery, stamps, guest registration cards, receipt book, etc.)
- real-time reservation service online
- legal and other professional fees
- utility deposits
- B&B association dues and fees

Your start-up list may include more or less depending on your property. If a property must be acquired, you will naturally have to include all of acquisition costs involved. I strongly suggest you research costs on every item, then estimate a little higher.

Notes:

Chapter Two
Your Road Map to Success: A Business Plan

Many individuals want to avoid writing this most important document. But if you are serious about this venture, you will not shy away from writing a business plan. It is a necessity.

You need a clear understanding of the business you desire to operate. You need to know its strengths and weaknesses long before you open the front door to welcome that first guest.

A simple business plan can be divided into four distinct sections, they are:

1. Description
2. Management
3. Marketing
4. Finances

Every business plan doesn't have to be complicated or filled with financial analysis that only a CPA can perform accurately. Many plans contain the four basic sections listed above, but all should do a good job of answering most of the 29 questions listed earlier.

One of the best ways to create a business plan is to review the plan of another bed and breakfast operation. Most state associations make sample business plans available to their members. Many hold workshops and seminars for Aspiring Innkeepers desiring assistance with the writing of their business plan.

The Small Business Administration has a sample B&B business plan on its Web site at www.sba.gov – it is comprehensive, well-written and available for study at no cost.

Know Your Community

As stated earlier, the location of your bed and breakfast establishment is important. This location includes the market area. If your community does not attract a sufficient number of overnight visitors, where will your guests come from?

Hospitality operations, which depend on tourists as part of their customer base, typically need local attractions to draw guests into their establishments. For this reason, it is very important to consider your local economics and demographics. What is the population growth in your community? What is the average local household income? What is the typical lifestyle of the local residents? What is the business climate like where you desire to establish bed and breakfast? The answers to all of these questions will assist you in identifying potential demand from local residents and business travelers.

It will be beneficial to investigate your local tourism trends, most Chamber of Commerce offices can assist you. Here are some trends to consider researching:

- Museum visitors
- Festivals & Local Events visitors
- Business visitors
- Local Attractions visitor count
- Boating activity
- Hunting and Fishing activity
- Golf Course usage
- College or University visitors
- Hospital or Medical Center visitors
- Fairgrounds visitors
- Antique collectors and shoppers
- Fine Art collectors and shoppers

Most communities have a room tax collection in place. You can often use the data from this municipal revenue stream as a gauge of local growth in lodging revenues. This same data can assist you in evaluating your competitors.

Know Your Competition

In order to be successful, bed and breakfast business owners must know their market, and this includes the competition. Competition can either be direct or indirect -- direct competition is a business offering bed and breakfast services to the type clientele; indirect competition is a lodging establishment with the similar service but appealing to a different type of client.

Studying your competitors can give you some of the most important market information you can gather for your business plan.

When evaluating your competition you want to closely analyze all your competitors – direct and indirect. Keep in mind, there are both advantages and disadvantages resulting from local competition. You must accept the fact that you may lose some guests to your competitors from time to time, but instead of being concerned with "what you could loose," we'll focus on "what you can gain" from both types of competition:

- Referrals
- Stronger destination image for your area
- Greater marketing power, especially if you co-operate with each other
- Greater community support
- Insight to pricing and the local hospitality market
- Ideas & advice from other B&B owners

Basically it comes down to this: the more you know about your competitors the better are your chances of success. Become familiar with competitor's daily room rates. Attempt to discover competitor's monthly and annual operating performance and occupancy rates. This information is not always easy to acquire, but very helpful if it can be obtained.

An in-depth study of the competition's strengths, weaknesses and competitive position in the marketplace is as important as occupancy rates. Here are some guidelines that will help you with your research:

- Does the competition require minimum stays? If the answer is yes, this usually means the operation can afford to be selective.
- What type of media coverage do area inns receive? Good coverage generally means local media considers these businesses vital to the community.
- Have existing B&Bs expanded in the recent past?
- Are the price ranges at all the area inns similar? Uniformly high price ranges generally indicate a prosperous marketplace.

Taking a tour of all the competitive lodging establishments is the best way to obtain first hand knowledge about each competitor's property. Develop a scoring system you are comfortable with and score each competitor on all of the following:

- Curb appeal
- Charm and uniqueness

- Exterior Condition
- Interior Condition
- Cleanliness
- Signage
- Parking for guests
- Local reputation
- Proximity to local attractions/activities
- Amenities

And, be sure you make a note of how many rooms offer private bathing or whirlpool tubs, and make note of the type and number of rooms available to guests.

As you gather the information on your competitors, be sure you transfer all of it into your business plan. Having bits and pieces of paper with data written on it in your purse, coat pockets and scattered on the kitchen counter is not going to do you much good. You need a well-organized written document that contains all your collected data in one place.

Be aware that we are only touching on the very basics of a business plan. I've met so many innkeepers operating with no written plan in place, so I feel it is better to have a basic plan than none at all. Having said this, let me encourage you to start with a basic plan and then continue building upon it as you become more and more familiar with the process.

A variety of studies have shown that business failures most often result from inadequate planning, financial pitfalls, excessive optimism, poor management, ineffective marketing, and ignoring the value of experience.

A business plan is a tool to help you effectively manage your business. Creating, constantly updating and following a good business plan could mean the difference between failure and success.

Our business plan helps us see where we have come from and what direction we're headed. (The bank loves when we have the data to back up our ideas.) This, however, does not mean that there have not been bumps and detours along the way, as a matter of fact, some of the detours have turned into many of our biggest blessings. We use our business plan to have goals that are put down on paper.

We start each year by asking what is the plan for this year, 2 years from now and 5 years from now. This year we have chosen a word that reflects our plan and it will be our theme for the year. It makes us ask ourselves, "How have we used our God given gift of hospitality and what can we do to share, promote and improve on that gift?"

Andrea and Merlynn Bean
Camp Bean Bed & Breakfast
4955 210th Avenue
Albert City, IA
www.campbeanbb.com

According to a study by the U. S. Small Business Association, only two-thirds of new small businesses survive at least two years, and just 44 percent survive at least four years. Writing and implementing a business plan can help you avoid becoming a start-up failure. A business plan forces you to think about the entire operation and come to terms with the businesses strengths and weaknesses. Innkeepers who do their homework and write a strong business plan increase their chances for business success.

Incompetence is the Main Cause of Failure

Research by Dun and Bradstreet clearly points out that failures result primarily from incompetence. Here are the reasons they list for B&B failures – in decreasing order:
1. Inadequate sales
2. Competitive weakness
3. Heavy operating expenses
4. Poor location
5. Excessive fixed costs
6. Problems related to poor judgment

Similarly, business and B&B consultants, like myself, claimed that 90% of business failures were due to management inadequacy (48% incompetence and 42% inexperience).

There are a variety of reasons why a small B&B can fail. There are some steps a new innkeeper can take to avoid the more obvious downfalls. Here are ten causes of B&B failure and how to avoid them.

1. Most new innkeepers don't have enough money saved up. Most experienced innkeepers I have spoken with on this topic agree that a new innkeeper needs to save up at least six months of worth living and business expenses prior to opening the door to serve the first guest. *(Pamela K. Adams, owner of the Metcalf House in Storm Lake, Iowa, had two years of savings in the bank before purchasing her established Victorian bed and breakfast.)*

2. Some inns don't advertise throughout the year. You must advertise in order for people to know about your lodging establishment. Having a Web site and belonging to a state bed and breakfast association are two of your most important advertising outlets.

3. Some inns fail due to low occupancy -- they just don't generate enough sales. Poor planning to begin with is often the direct cause of low occupancy. If the doors are still open, it's not too late to put a strong marketing plan into action. The Internet will provide you with low cost marketing. If you included a blog on the same server with your Web site, discipline yourself

to blog daily posting local events and special lodging package or hot deals. Write a press release and distribute it online via one PRWeb.com. Spend a day delivering your brochure or rack card to every attraction, real estate office, beauty parlor and funeral home in your community. Take another day and go to every hotel, motel and B&B operation in your community asking for referral business on the days they are full. Keep this marketing focus until you begin to see an increase in sales.

4. The innkeeper can't survive during the slow season off the inn alone, so often, a B&B will fail due to low occupancy. Again planning is the key, but if you find yourself in this situation, you need to find alternative income streams to generate enough sales or save up enough money during the busy season to survive during the slow season.

5. The innkeeper doesn't have enough money to keep a professional image. Most companies lose sales when they don't look professional or even stay professional in appearance. This road to failure is seen much too often within the industry! It is okay to be frugal in this business, but doing everything on the cheap is a different story. Watch for sales on everything from

lounging robes, to soap to Web design services – this keep expenses down, but not quality or professional image.

6. Violating city rules or state regulations is one way to go out of business quickly. You need to follow city rules and follow the state regulations otherwise you won't have a business.

Topics to Include in the Basic Business Plan

The first step in the development process of drafting a business plan is creating a list of the critical topics you must be sure to include. Many business ideas fail because they were not logically planned.

A business plan is the foundation upon which all your business decisions will be based. T his includes the four sections mentioned previously:

1. Description: A basic description of your proposed B&B
2. Management: Operations related goals and objectives
3. Marketing: How you plan to become successful
4. Finances: Where money will come from and how it will be managed – this section includes the projected income stream of the business

A business plan defines why you are in business, what your market is, what your strengths and weaknesses are, and your financial management environment. The plan will help you make insightful business decisions and inform potential lenders about your business. To develop a reliable business plan, you will need to review other successful B&B plans. You will find a list of resources at the end of this chapter or you may be able to obtain samples from the small business development center in your region.

The following areas need special attention and you should be sure all of these sections appear in your plan, you might say these are the elements of a simple basic B&B business plan.

Occupancy and Revenue Forecasting

This is your first serious look at the potential of the lodging establishment you are considering. Accurately forecasting sales revenue is an extremely difficult task. Your perception of future revenue will be your guide when you forecast expenses and plan the overall operation.

The projected income includes all revenues from the operation, plus any other revenue such as interested earned on CDs or bank accounts. The most important projection will be that of room sales. You calculate this projection by multiplying the number of rooms rented during a given period by the room rate. Since most bed and breakfast operations include breakfast in the room rate, you must take this into consideration when setting your room rates. If you have a computer, you can use a spreadsheet program to make the task of projecting cash flow much easier.

As you get into projecting and analyzing cash flow, you will first need to determine the breakeven occupancy so that you know the very minimum at which the B&B should operate.

Normally, negative cash flow is created when a property collects less income than is needed to pay all the outgoing bills. A key component that greatly affects breakeven occupancy rate is the amount of debt service. (Usually in the form of a monthly mortgage payment.) A property with a large percentage of debt usually has a high breakeven point thus creating much more risk to cash flow.

In order to determine if your B&B has a high chance of success, you must forecast your sales revenue by predicting the number of rooms you will rent during a future period and multiplying that number by the room rate. Predicting the number of rooms you will rent is often difficult for a new B&B, because the indicator is the data available on past occupancy in your area -- an element you can research, but will have to guess at unless you can obtain solid data from a local hotel, motel, or B&B owner.

Occupancy is the measure of the percentage of available rooms that were actually rented. The occupancy rate during your first year will depend on many factors, these include your area, the uniqueness of your B&B, and the amount of promotional activity you undertake. Usually the occupancy rates for new B&B operations are roughly 30-40 percent of the average occupancy rate of the hotels and motels in the surrounding community. Some of our rural Iowa B&Bs average as low as 15 percent occupancy during the first year. The establishments with this low of an occupancy rate usually did not plan ahead and did not obtain a strong Web site presence at least six months prior to opening the doors.

The best advice I can give you on this element of your business plan is to really work with these numbers and don't skip over this portion of the planning process.

Start-up Costs

Start-up costs are a critical component of your B&B business plan. Even if your home is paid for and know you can be ready for guests quickly, most properties will need some improvements to create an ideal B&B experience.

First, sit down and make a list of all the expenses you believe you will incur in order to accept the first guest's reservation request. At minimum, be sure you include annual dues for the state B&B association, food and beverage expenses, cost of B&B specialty insurance, projected maintenance and repairs, all your room and housekeeping supplies, cost for new towels and linens, and any new technology you may need to effectively operative – this includes the cost of real-time online reservation service, a computer, a fax machine, and any software/training needed.

Your estimated expenses will help you determine if the B&B concept you have in mind will be profitably.

Keep in mind that your start-up costs will be based on the type of experience you want your guests to have. For the most part, B&B operations provide lodging for the evening and breakfast in the room rate. However, trends are changing and many new innkeepers are offering their guests more privacy by delivering a tray or breakfast basket to the room. Some are now offering a check-in snack or evening snack. The Country Connection Bed & Breakfast in Prairie City, Iowa, offers homemade ice cream in the evenings. No matter what services you offer, you'll need to calculate expenses and add them to your business plan.

When projecting expenses, don't forget you'll need marketing materials. Be sure you include the cost of creating and printing, business cards, rack cards, stationery, envelopes and outdoor signage which will identify your B&B business.

You also need to consider your business office area and its needs. In the 21st Century, innkeepers can't get along without a personal computer system and printer to handle reservations (online and off), maintain financial records, and to support online marketing activities. There is always the exception to this, but it will most likely be a start-up with fewer than 4 rooms. Using computer technology to manage your business finances will save you a lot of time and money. In most cases the technology will make you money!

If you join a state B&B association that assigns mentors, you may want to consider having your mentor review your costs list. If you have missed an important item, they should be able to alert you. If your mentor is from your immediate community, they could make sure you have considered costs you might incur due to local fire and health ordinance requirements.

Include Your Operations Strategy

During your planning stage, it is essential that you develop an operating plan for the business to insure that it will run smoothly. Identify and determine how you implement procedures for handling the day-to-day operation of the business, including B&B policies, finances, facility maintenance, food preparation/service, and guest relations.

If you are developing your business plan to use as a supporting document when requesting a loan, be sure to include short bios of each B&B team member and the expertise they bring to the operation.

Marketing Is an Essential Element of Any Business Plan

Two of the biggest mistakes new B&B owners often make are 1) thinking that everyone will want to stay at their accommodation and buy whatever they are selling, and 2) thinking that their property will sell itself because it is so unique and wonderful. A detailed business plan will help eliminate both of these mistakes. In later chapters you will find detailed professional tips for marketing your B&B both online and off.

Turn All Activities Into Marketing Opportunities

Marketing is a never-ending process. Learn to think in terms of "marketing" — no matter where you are and no matter what you are doing. Always carry marketing materials with you. Taking a ride on an elevator in a local department store? Chat with the folks standing next to you, and if they seem interested in your operation hand them a business card or some other appropriate piece of printed marketing material – brochure, rack card, etc.

Jane Lawhead, innkeeper at Charlie-Jane's Bed & Breakfast in Mt. Ayr, Iowa, works a full time job at a local hospital. Jane keeps copies of her B&B brochure in her purse or tote so that no matter where she is at, if the subject of lodging arises she has printed materials available to give out.

A Web site is almost a necessity in the 21st Century. The Internet is quickly becoming the preferred method of planning travel. Know "ahead of time" how you're going to market it to potential guests. Getting your marketing plan down on paper and included in your business plan is the best way to focus on exactly how you will sell your specific B&B experience.

In your marketing plan, outline how you will utilize E-mail Marketing. E-mail gives you on-going opportunities, at a very low cost, to keep prospective guests and faithful returning guests up-to-date about the activities, events and lodging packages your B&B is offering. Compare the cost of e-mail marketing to the cost of newspaper, magazine or direct mail, where readers often never see your ad, and you'll realize how important this form of communication is to your inn's success. Constant Contact (www.constantcontact.com) and services like it are inexpensive and they offer powerful e-mail marketing potential to their subscribers.

I wrote a business plan and it was vital for several reasons, they include:

1. It allowed me to decide whether or not to [take out a bank loan] to move ahead with the business.

2. It informed the bank of why I wanted to borrow the money to furnish the building.

3. Whenever I have a lull with the business it provides me with a list of goals and things I need to do to achieve those goals so that a lull never gets me down. (Instead it is an opportunity to return to the plan and keep moving forward).

4. It also shows me how far I have come with the business, which along with the many satisfied customers, are really the shot in the arm that keeps me going.

Liz Norton
Historic Lincoln Hotel
408 Main Street, Box 222
Lowden, IA 52255
www.lincolnhoteliowa.com

Resources for Writing the Bed & Breakfast Business Plan

How to Open a Financially Successful Bed & Breakfast or Small Hotel (Paperback) by Lora Arduser and Douglas R. Brown
Paperback: 283 pages
Publisher: Atlantic Publishing Company (FL); Paperback/CD edition (May 2004)
ISBN-10: 0910627304
ISBN-13: 978-0910627306
Product Dimensions: 8 x 5.2 x 0.8 inches
$39.95
    This is a comprehensive handbook with companion CD ROM that has an actual business plan you can use and edit in MS Word. This book does a good job of explaining how to set up and operate a financially successful bed-and-breakfast or small hotel.

The Business Planning Guide (Paperback) by David H. Bangs
Paperback: 256 pages
Publisher: Kaplan Business; 9 edition (May 15, 2002)
ISBN-10: 079315409X
ISBN-13: 978-0793154098
Product Dimensions: 11 x 8.6 x 0.6 inches
$24.95
    This is a good basic book for anyone considering a business start-up and preparing to write a business plan. It has sound advice and step-by-step strategies needed to compile a complete business plan and/or financing proposal It does not focus on the hospitality industry, but it covers sound basic financial principals and the art of writing and implementing a business plan. After all, a business plan won't do anyone much good if it is never put into action.

So - You Want to Be an Innkeeper (Paperback)
by Jo Ann M. Bell, Susan Brown, Mary Davies, and Pat Hardy
Paperback: 336 pages
Publisher: Chronicle Books; 4 Rev Exp edition (March 2004)
ISBN-10: 0811841103
ISBN-13: 978-0811841108
Product Dimensions: 8.9 x 6 x 0.9 inches
$16.95

This is a reliable source of information for anyone getting ready to begin a career as a B&B owner. Charts and worksheets for financial planning, property evaluation, and cash flow projections are included. This is a B&B resource guide every innkeeper should have in their library.

How to Open and Operate a Bed & Breakfast, 8th
(Paperback)
by Jan Stankus
Paperback: 384 pages
Publisher: Globe Pequot; Eighth edition edition (January 1, 2007)
ISBN-10: 0762741759
ISBN-13: 978-0762741755
Product Dimensions: 9.1 x 7.5 x 0.9 inches
$18.95

This book has lots of practical advice written in easy to understand terms. It also includes a Worksheet for Start-up Expenses and an Appendix of Web-based Resources.

Determining Room Prices

One of your most difficult tasks as a new innkeeper will be setting your room rates. The rates you charge should be fair, reasonable and competitive but still allow you to make a reasonable profit.

As you might expect, the keyword above is "reasonable." You can charge whatever rate you want, but if you pull your room rates out of the air and the potential guests perceive them as overpriced you may find yourself out of business before you really get started.

It is also important to project expenses from start-up to the time you will reach break even occupancy level. If there are no reserves in the bank for losses during the start-up period until you break even, bankruptcy could occur. It is not at all out of line to plan for it to take two or more years to generate a profit.

There are many factors influencing a reasonable market rate for any given bed and breakfast operation. These factors include: location, area population, type of operation, size of establishment, amenities, local lodging competition, proximity to a known tourist attraction, operational expenses, insurance rates, cost of advertising, proximity to local attractions and activities, presences on the Internet, and much more.

Examining what others are charging for similar rooms and services will guide you when you're figuring out what a "fair market price" would be for your operation. You will also find it useful to conduct a Breakeven Analysis.

A breakeven analysis is used to determine how much sales volume your business needs in order to start making a profit. The breakeven analysis will help you develop a reasonable pricing strategy for your business plan. To conduct a breakeven analysis, use this formula:

Fixed Costs *divided* by Revenue per room *minus* the Variable Costs per room

Fixed costs are the ones that must be paid whether or not any of your rooms are rented. These costs are "fixed" over a specified period of time.

Variable costs are ones that vary in direct proportion with sales or revenues -- the higher the occupancy, the higher the cost. Generally innkeepers would consider the costs of food, laundry, linen, and guest supplies to be a variable cost. Knowing how many guest days (or dollars) are necessary to cover your costs is extremely important. You are highly encouraged to add a "break-even-chart" or "profit graph" of some sort to your business plan. Granted, it will take additional time and energy to prepare, but the benefit of this type of financial aid is well worth the time and energy it will take to produce.

Many new innkeepers have been known to place this type of a visual on a wall near their desk or post it on their personal use refrigerator right next to their children's school photos.

The break-even chart, or profit graph, indicates how sales volume, selling price, and operating expenses affect profits and how many room sales are necessary to achieve before you will begin to make a profit. Consult hospitality financial and accounting textbooks for more information on this important topic.

Determining your rates can become a complex and involved activity, especially when you begin creating package deals and seasonal rate schedules. But, no mater what rates you determine work best for your property, in your specific location, be sure the potential guests can easily understand them.

Guests tend to expect higher room rates in larger cities and for those near well-known tourism activities.

One requirement for IBBIA membership is that the cost for breakfast, which varies from inn to inn, be included in the guest's room rate. Increases in guest room rates are influenced by: private baths, private in-room whirlpool tubs, antique beds, feather beds, full breakfasts by candlelight, evening desserts, softened water, seating space in gardens, location near water, two beds in a room, etc.

Creative styles of service: guests making their own breakfast, buffet style, family style, served on the patio or deck.

Decorating and themes: heart-shaped whirlpools, rose petals on beds, rocks surrounding the whirlpools, cottages, cabins, carriage houses, antique jails, "rent-a-cat" for the night in your room, grandma-type antiques in rooms can all affect your guest room rates. Also keep in mind the need to adjust rates as the market conditions and your establishment change.

Mary Nichols, President IBBIA
Hannah Marie Country Inn
4070 Hwy. 71
Spencer, IA 51301
www.hannahmarieinn.com

Leave No Stone Unturned

Every bed and breakfast has its own style and ambience. The best consistently weave the character and overall mood of the inn throughout every aspect of the operation, be it Victorian Mansion or a Jail House Inn. Planned style and ambience can result in an essential marketing tool over the lifetime of the inn, but the details important to a guest must not be overlooked for the sake of style.

Make Sure you Prioritize the Needs of Your Guests

Sometimes, boasting about what you do, or plan to do, you're your guests is meaningless if you're not focused on what the customer really wants or needs. Guests may enjoy the unique and different style you've created, but if there is no place to hang their clothes when they arrive in their assigned rooms, you have failed to meet the needs of the guests.

You don't have to be a mind reader to figure out what is best for your guests. This is where planning comes in. The task of creating something unique and functional starts with dealing with and meeting guest expectations.

Research and know the industry expectations. Your state B&B association can be a great assistance or if your state does not have an organized and active educational program, you can contact the Professional Association of Innkeepers International (PAII). You can find information about PAII online at www.paii.org or you can write to them at their Headquarters in New Jersey at 207 White Horse Pike, Haddon Heights, NJ 08035 or call them at 800.468.PAII (7244) or 856.310.1102. PAII often publishes industry statistics online, and they also have detailed industry research available for sale.

Learn From Experienced Innkeepers

Travel and stay at B&Bs – paying attention to all the details. Let the innkeepers know you are planning to open your own establishment and ask for one piece of sage advice. Most will be very helpful, and a few will not, but you have nothing to loose and everything to gain.

As you visit other inns, make written notes as you analyze how their approaches work or miss the mark. Take away and adapt ideas that you feel will enhance your operation. Visit other inns with an open mind – if you arrive speaking and acting like a "know-it-all" don't expect a seasoned innkeeper to share, after all, how could they help someone that already "knows all there is to know." Be humble, ask your host to share, and be open to hearing the opinions and tips your hosts are offering. Take what you feel will be helpful from your conversations and politely ignore anything that doesn't fit into your goals and objectives.

Inn Travelers are Unique

People who stay at bed and breakfasts aren't ordinary travelers. They're looking for quality lodging and service, as well as the uniqueness of each B&B and each innkeeper. What may work for one innkeeper may not necessarily work for another.

As you complete your research, keep in mind that B&B guests generally aren't looking for a bargain. In fact, they're often willing to pay more for something different and out of the ordinary. (Which doesn't necessarily mean that discounts and special packages aren't an effective way of marketing bed and breakfasts.)

As you plan for the startup of your bed and breakfast, you'll need to make some decisions in order for the experience to be both profitable for you and enjoyable for your guests. Again, the importance of writing a business plan and implementing it can't be stressed enough.

Several things come to mind when I am asked what innkeepers should place high on their list of priorities. Recently, my husband and I stayed at a lovely B&B in a neighboring state. The inn was beautifully restored, filled with period antiques, the innkeepers very friendly, and the breakfasts delicious. Our room was very comfortable, well decorated, and featured a four-poster king-sized bed. However, one area that was slighted was the bathroom. The attached bathroom (formerly a closet) had a nice shower, a small sink, and a clothes hook, but no towel bars, no place to put your travel items, one bar of soap (which was in the shower), no other amenities, and the towels were located on a small stand in the bedroom. What do I remember about our stay? All of the good things, but also the lack of bathroom amenities we all take for granted.

Leslie Schultz
The Gardner House
400 Western Street
Lost Nation, Iowa 52254
www.thegardnerhousebandb.com

Loyalty Programs

No business is perfect; there's always room for improvement. While in the planning stage, consider the various loyalty programs that might work well for your type of operation.

The use of Internet technologies provide new opportunities in the transfer of information between the guest and the innkeeper that did not exist a few years ago. Guest loyalty can be continually optimized as new technologies emerge. Information can be distributed at a faster pace and with a greater degree of efficiency. With appropriate technology you can expand on the basic details known about your guests. Do they prefer a room with a tub/shower combination or one with a double whirlpool tub, do they prefer a full breakfast in the dining room or one served on a tray to their room. The objective is to know your guests' needs so as to be able to exceed all expectations.

The best loyalty programs for B&Bs are personalized. They are all about the customer -- their needs, their likes and their expectations. The goal is to exceed guest expectations. It is also very important to target specific markets. Each market has different needs and trends and you should be recognizing and meeting these needs.

Technology is the base for success in a loyalty program, but it changes quickly in this new technology age so you must be prepared to make changes as the trends change. E-mail marketing and online surveys can help you establish an ongoing dialogue with your guests. They can also help you build the relationship and grow your business.

E-mail marketing is so popular because:

- sending e-mail is much cheaper than most other forms of communication
- e-mail lets you deliver your message directly to the individual (unlike a Web site, where the people have to come to your message)
- email marketing has proven very successful for those who do it right

Once you are open and operating, realize there is a reason you have loyal guests returning year after year to your inn. These guests like doing business with you, and they'll like you even more if you ask their opinion..

Women make particularly excellent sources of information and opinion. With a highly connected brain-wiring configuration, women have a heightened sensory awareness and notice the finest of details. Their suggestion of a subtle change in the way you do business can mean the difference between ordinary profit and miraculous growth.

A Cancellation Policy Belongs in Your Business Plan

Every bed and breakfast inn needs a cancellation policy that is unique to the establishment. The policy will ultimately be placed on the majority of your marketing materials, your Web site and the confirmation email or letter sent out. It is also a good idea to include the cancellation policy on any reservation form the guest fills-out prior to or upon arrival. Since this policy goes on so many documents, it is best to have a cancellation policy that is explainable in simple, clear terms.

Most hotels and motels have cancellation policies that allow a refund if the expected guest cancels forty-eight hours prior to the reservation date. Few bed and breakfast establishments can afford to follow this type of policy, because they do not do the volume of business a hotel or motel with 30 or more rooms might do. Most bed and breakfast operations will require cancellation notice starting at 7 days, and it is not uncommon for an inn to require a 20 day notice.

Also, be aware that most bed and breakfast inns require a credit card number to secure a reservation. If the guest does not cancel the reservation within the cancellation notice period and does not arrive at the B&B, the innkeeper will charge the credit card for the first night's accommodation. Without a credit card the innkeeper risks being left with an empty room, perhaps with declined requests from other potential guests.

While it is important to have a simple, but clear cancellation policy, it is just as important to be understanding if there is a death, serious illness, or if severe weather causes a guest to make a last minute cancellation. You will not regret offering this type of consideration to your guests as it builds goodwill, which really is priceless to a small business. You can always mail a distressed guest, cancelling at the last minute, a gift certificate for a future visit equal to the amount of the deposit they lost. This makes the guest feel good and builds goodwill for your operation.

You will also need to establish a cancellation policy for early check-outs. Here is an example of a well-written early check-out policy:

> "Early check-outs will be charged the full rate for the room, unless it is re-rented by 9:00 p.m."

Other cancellation topics you will need to address in your business plan will be special event bookings, group bookings, special lodging packages and groups booking your entire property for a wedding, reception or other celebration. Here is an example of group event check-out policy: "In the event you have requested a room within the groups reserved rooms and check out prior to your reserved check-out date, the innkeeper will add an early check-out fee of $100.00 to your individual account. If we wish to avoid an early checkout fee, you should advise the innkeeper at or before check-in of any change in planned length of stay."

Accepting Credit Cards can be Considered Insurance

Because of the rising cost of accepting credit cards at a bed and breakfast, some innkeepers elect not to accept them. These innkeepers tend to believe they are "saving money and cutting down on expenses." Unfortunately, it is the farthest thing from the truth of the matter. A change of attitude is necessary.

Think of credit cards as if you were paying for insurance, because in reality it is one of the best uses of a guest's credit card. Consider the damage that two drunken adults in a heated argument could do to your property in a matter of minutes. If you don't have a credit card on file for one of them, and both of them have given you false contact information, how in the world will you replace the stained carpet, broken chairs or other expensive damage they have done to your room?

Obviously I've taken an extreme situation that seldom happens at a bed and breakfast establishment to illustrate my point, but it is not an unheard of occurrence. It could happen. If you have their credit card on file, you have recourse as well as correct contact information for at least one of them.

I will not take one credit card for a group. I ask the group leader to have each couple call me separately or book online separately. Then if they need to cancel within the cancellation period, I issue them an e-mail future stay certificate numbered the same as their original reservation confirmation/cancellation notice. This certificate is not valid for football game weekends, graduation, or holidays and is not transferable. This e-mail certificate must be presented at time of check in. There is no expiration date but the certificate will be valid for the stated amount and if they want to upgrade, they can pay the difference.

Nila Haug
The Golden Haug
517 East Washington
Iowa City, IA 52240
www.goldenhaug.com

Chapter Three
Marketing a B&B in the 21st Century

The computer is as much a part of everyday life in the 21st Century as cell phones, fax machines and portable DVDs. At the end of March 2006, 42% of Americans had high-speed at home, up from 30% in March 2005, or a 40% increase. And 48 million Americans -- mostly those with high-speed access at home – say they have posted content to the Internet. (*The Pew Research Center, May 2006.*)

According to a report released by www.TravelCLICK.net, slightly over 37% of all Central Reservation Office reservations for major hotel brands were made via the Internet in the second quarter of 2006, nearly 20% more than in the same period of 2005.

And if these numbers aren't staggering enough for you, consider the fact that online travel spending is about to make a significant dent in the billion-dollar travel industry with over $125 billion in total spending on the Internet by the year 2011 (By comparison, 2006 accumulated $49 billion.)

As you should clearly see from these facts, marketing your bed and breakfast establishment online is essential to the success of your inn. While Internet marketing has a learning curve of its own, you also need to realize that practically all traditional marketing basics apply to the Internet.

So the best place to begin a discussion on marketing a bed and breakfast in the 21st Century starts with a discussion on the basics.

Marketing Materials Must Send a Consistent Message

Now more than ever, it's critical to deliver an effective message efficiently—and in a clear, consistent manner that speaks to your guest's needs. An integrated or coordinated marketing approach ensures your lodging establishment is sending a consistent message throughout all of your marketing materials -- whether it be a brochure, a Web site, a seasonal promo, a newspaper advertisement, or a press release. The challenge is to create professional materials with the same consistent "look" and "feel" both in print and online. The ultimate goal of your message is to have it **Recognized, Received and Remembered!**

Start with your story. You need to create a powerful 30 second message that is compelling on both an emotional and logical level. It must inspire and motivate the prospective guest to action, as well as answer the question: 'What do I get for my money?'

Your 30 Second Message

When people approach you and you have the opportunity to introduce yourself, include your name and your occupation, you want to think in terms of a TV or radio commercial. Most of them are just 30 seconds. And, in that short 30 seconds the commercial sells a product or service. You should be able to sell yourself and your Bed and Breakfast in 30 seconds or less.

Take the time to put together a 30-second sales pitch that tells who you are and what your accommodations have to offer a potential guest. Practice your commercial over and over until it rolls out of your mouth without conscious thought.

This 30 second message is also the foundation for all your marketing materials. It can incorporate a motto such as, "Back Inn Time Bed and Breakfast: you'll love going back" or it can toot your own horn as in this example: "Hannah Marie Country Inn, an award winning bed and breakfast."

And, if your personality lends itself toward humor, and the property fits the message, you might build your pitch around an aspect of your property: "Jailhouse Inn, a bed and breakfast worth going to jail for!"

Here is an example of a good solid 30 second message given to me – without a great deal of thought – by a seasoned innkeeper:

I am Dr. Marie Brady, owner of Victoria Bed and Breakfast Inn and Studios in Fort Madison, Iowa. Our unique historical Inn is located on the banks of the Mississippi River, in the midst of the most significant historical restoration site west of the Hudson. We look forward to sharing our unique architecture and hospitality.

Here is another example for you to consider, this one is from an innkeeper with over 20 years of experience:

Hello. I'm Mary Nichols, an innkeeper. A passionate one. You know, the kind of innkeeper who centers upon your needs. AND pays attention to the smallest of details: rose petals sprinkled on your bed, softened water and bubbles for your private in-room whirlpool, a cloud of goose down to sleep under, evening chocolate desserts by the glow of candlelight, a light breakfast brought to your guestroom door. I'm that kind of innkeeper. Come, experience the Hannah Marie Country Inn.

A great place to practice your 30-second message is at social functions. Once you have your story down, get out to more events and network with people. Find out when the next Chamber of Commerce networking event is taking place and attend. That means dress up and show up! Your message can't be **Recognized, Received and Remembered** if it the public never hears it.

Because it is also important to not take everything in life so drop-dead-serious, your message, once fine-tuned and put into regular use, can be adjusted to fit whatever situation or environment. Here is a great example of a humorous message that will work as a great ice breaker in some social settings:

Hi - I'm Nila Haug, owner, innkeeper, bed maker and toilet scrubber for the past 17 years of A Bed and Breakfast the Golden Haug in Iowa City, Iowa.

You Need a Loud Marketing Voice

Once you have your message, it's time to give thought to your marketing voice. Most innkeepers tend to work with relatively small marketing budgets. (Nationally this number is usually around 5% of the entire operating budget – for this reason, seasoned innkeepers sing-out-at-the-top-of-their-voice when it comes to marketing!) A smaller budget might reduce the volume of your marketing voice, but it doesn't have to reduce its quality. To get your message through with the clarity of a string quartet, start by analyzing what your current message is saying to your potential guests:

- ***Does your message tell a potential guest what you have to offer?*** More times than you might expect, innkeeper messages don't really say anything at all, at least not anything a potential guest cares about. Cut through the noise by basing your message on what you know about the needs of guests.
- ***Does your message say the same thing every time?*** Consistency is crucial, particularly in noisy, crowded marketing environments. Are your printed materials, online communications and everything else in harmony? If yes, then, resist the urge to change your message just because you're tired of it -- you hear it a thousand times more often than your potential guests. Remember, the goal of your message is to be **Recognized, Received and Remembered!**

Your Logo is Important

Your story is ready, so it's time to move on to your logo and then work through the various materials that are most important to you as an innkeeper.

At the risk of sounding corny and boring, I'm going to stress the fact that we rarely get a second chance to make a first impression. The first impression, regardless of the nature of the encounter, is a lasting perception. With fierce competition within some lodging markets today, the "out of the gate" success of any new business will be greatly influenced by the strength of its perceived image. Before any new business opens its doors or Web site, it's important for the physical or graphic image to be purposeful, professional and clear. Again, the objective is to be **Recognized, Received and Remembered**!

Your logo becomes the essence of your inn's image. It is your calling card. It will become subliminally synonymous with your business -- think of big red K or the golden arches. Most Americans have immediate recall and awareness – K-Mart and McDonalds. Concentrate on the lasting, emotional cues of your business, such as quality, reliability, style or history.

Consider working with professionals to develop your inn's business identity. You are looking at a one time cost that can serve you well for many years.

Opt for an Effective Logo – Not the Most Ornate

When working with a graphic designer, opt for the most effective presentation – which isn't always the most ornate.

Once you have your logo, and know your color palette, place your logo in all your marketing materials – from business cards to stationary, to brochures, to signage, to rack cards, to local advertising, to your Web site and, of course, on all your guest-related materials.

About Out-of-Date Logos

If you are the operator of an existing inn, unless there has been a strategic shift in your inn's vision or ownership, a logo should stand the test of time with minor updating. A well-established inn may consider their original logo to be outdated or a drag on their attempts to attract a younger more affluent contemporary customer. If this is the case, then yes, by all means give your entire orchestra of marketing materials a new upbeat rhythm.

Working With a Graphic Artist

If your budget for marketing materials is limited, do your best not to pinch-pennies when it comes to working with a graphic artist on your logo. Your logo is going to appear on all your marketing materials – from the sign in the front yard to your letterhead, ads, brochures, postcards, soaps, and all other marketing materials you create over time.

Angie Roberts, an award winning graphic artist and owner of Graphic Details, has the following advice regarding logo design:

Think outside the box, think long term, think simple. A logo (ie Nike swoosh) should be able to grow with your company and not limit marketing potential, therefore abstract is often a good choice. Have your graphic designer do 3 totally different designs so you can judge for yourself what will work in the long term and what might be too limiting.

Be sure the format your designer is creating will allow you to size your logo from very, very small (on a ball point pen) to very, very large (a trade show back drop or billboard). This is called a "vector format" and artwork created this way is scalable to any size without losing quality. (Again, think long term...just because your company/organization does not do trade shows or have a billboard today does not mean you never will.)

And then while making the final decision; remember it's all about image! Don't look at your logo image through your eyes but rather through the eyes of the potential guests you are hoping will stay at your inn. Be sure to consider how your target audience will perceive your company through that first introductory marketing event — whether it's through a business card in person or via the Worldwide Web – it's all important. You never get to make a first impression twice! So make it a good one!

Seek out graphic designers with experience in the hospitality industry. Review their previous work and be sure their style fits-in with your ideas and visions. Obtain prices and get a clear understanding of how they work with clients. It is often helpful if you can show them a sketch of what you have in mind and some idea of the style of font you'd like to see used.

Be cautious when thinking about hiring a close friend or a family member. Your new venture's professional image is critical to the future success of your business, it must be easy to make clear choices and say no without being concerned over hurting a friend or family member's feelings.

Copy and How it Addresses the Desirable Details of Your Location

Interesting content should be the basis of any marketing piece. It is important to select and edit your work – and, again, I suggest you consider hiring a professional to do it for you.

Traditional methods of advertising goods and services work. They work in print and they work on the Internet. They are proven techniques that have, and still are, moving billions of boxes of hardware and widgets around the world. And they are methods which have been practiced and finely tuned for over a century.

I was extremely lucky to have taught at the Dale Carnegie training facility in Houston, Texas. The experience changed my life forever. I will be eternally grateful for the many things I learned from my students. At the top of the list is persistence, goal setting and to trust in my own process.

From the Carnegie system I learned to apply the **'3 Rs:** The **R**ight words, in the **R**ight order, to the **R**ight person. And do it with a smile!

It's over 22 years since I learned those 'right words', and I've never looked back. A few years after leaving Houston, someone else showed me how to do exactly the same thing with the **written word**. It's called copywriting. **The power of the pen**.

If you're really serious about learning how to write effective response-driven sales copy that will **substantially** increase your profits, I recommend you do the following:

- Read as much as you can about Copywriting, Marketing, Advertising, and Selling. Remember this: despite what some may say about writing for the Web, most of the winning copywriting techniques being successfully applied in the print media today are just as effective on the Web. There are some important differences in presentation. But, the sales psychology is the same.
- There are four 'triggers' when writing your copy that you need to keep in the forefront of your mind: *Attention. Interest. Desire. Action.*
- Never forget: The goal of your message is to be **Recognized, Received and Remembered!**

The Essential Elements of Successful Sales Copy

- THE HEADLINE grabs the reader's attention.
- THE SUBHEAD reinforces the main heading.
- THE ILLUSTRATION or PHOTO emphasizes the headline benefit.

- THE BODY COPY starts with a compelling paragraph that leads the reader in to the next section – often referred to as your "hook."
- THE FURTHER PARAGRAPHS support and reinforce the benefits of the offer.
- THE SECOND TO LAST PARAGRAPH warns the reader of the consequences of missing out on the offer.
- THE FINAL PARAGRAPH stimulates response. (Make your reservation now!)

Web pages require a slightly different technique, but the overall principle is still the same: Grab Attention, Stimulate Interest, Build up Desire, Urge the reader into Action!

The Importance of Carrying the Message to the Internet

Research has shown that over half of new inn guests are now coming from the Internet, and it is projected that over 90% of all new bookings will be made online in 2007. Focus needs to be shifted to your Web site.

Good Web sites Don't Call Attention to Themselves

In 2005, I visited a friend's new home in Seattle. And ever since my friend moved to this house, she has bragged about the view from her living room's large picture window that looks into a massive yard filled with mature trees, striking exotic flowers and lots of wild life that she feeds regularly.

The yard was everything she said, beautiful, peaceful and filled with friendly creatures. Once inside the house, however, she led me to the picture window. The yard remained spectacular, but, you barely noticed it. The inside of the window was dusty and there were fingerprints all over. The outside of the window was a target for bird droppings. It was difficult to ignore the window in order to appreciate the yard.

Don't let your Web site have much in common with this window. Your visitors come to your Web site to accomplish something -- to research, to price your accommodations, or to make a reservation. Your site's goal is to become transparent -- just like a clean, well-built window.

A window that's cracked, or dirty, hung too high or too low only calls attention to itself. It doesn't allow people to see past it and fully appreciate the view.

A Web site that's inadequately planned and poorly executed, or a mystery to navigate, doesn't allow visitors to accomplish what they've come to do. The site calls attention to itself and not the view it's offering. Often, visitors will move on to your competition's site because yours may not be helping them accomplish what they came to do.

A frustrating experience with your Web site tells visitors that they'll probably have a frustrating experience doing business with you. A clean, efficient site tells visitors that you have a clean, efficient business. Here are some simple rules that will help you create a Web site in harmony with your goal to be **Recognized, Received and Remembered.**

Tell Your Story on Your Web site

My clients have seen solid results from this practice so I feel confident in telling you to use the same copy for your brochures and your Web site. You can refer inquiring guests to your Web site for more information on certain subjects appearing in your brochure. That creates a seamless link between your print and online communications. Use this step as a catalyst to also link your press releases, and other print materials to your Web site. The possibilities are endless.

- **Avoid repeating yourself:** Having text that repeats the picture content - it should offer new information or place the picture in a new context.

- **Fast access is vital:** Research shows that if your site doesn't load in 20 seconds most people will give up.

- **Content is Critical:** Provide only the amount of content needed to help your visitor reach his or her goal. People do not like to read volumes on a Web site. Reading from computer screens is about **25% slower** than reading from paper.

- **Computer Screens Hurt the Eyes:** You should write 50% less text than you would for print. And, visitors don't like to scroll: one more reason to keep pages short.

- **Skimming instead of reading is a fact of the Web**: It has been confirmed by countless usability studies. Web writers have to acknowledge this fact and write for scan ability.

- **The Site Must Flow:** Get your message out when the home page first loads. Links to your rooms and the grounds will draw visitors into the site. Give people all the options to contact you. Be sure every page has a prominent link to a contact page. If you leave off an e-mail address because you do not want spammers to obtain it, provide a form where a message can be forwarded to your e-mail account.

- **High Quality Photos Are a Must:** If your visitors can see good quality photographs of your inn on the Internet, they are much more likely to want to book a reservation.

- **Be Inviting:** The site needs to be pleasant to view and easy to navigate. Maintain a consistent look and feel that mirrors your brochure.

- **Provide Support:** A huge factor in the success of your Web site depends on you answering e-mail inquiries. If visitors send you e-mails and you do not return them in a timely fashion, you have lost a customer and your competitor down the road has gained one.

- **Showcase Your B&B, not Your Designer:** Your site is about your inn, your services and/or your products. If your designer does not appear to understand this, find a new designer. If you utilize the services of a web development firm that specializes in lodging properties, you will seldom have this problem. These designers know exactly what a lodging property needs to have on a Web site to create a site that performs well on the Internet.

- **Include a Call to Action:** There is a precise point in the content delivery where you must include a call to action. The objective is to get a prospective guest to contact you for more information or make an online reservation so you can realize your goal to have your message **Recognized, Received and Remembered.**

Importance of Color and Photography on the Web

No discussion about a Web site is complete without discussing color and photography. Colors do not load on a Web page - text and graphics load. Color is nothing more than a text string six characters long. "Web Safe" colors come the closest to looking the same on every monitor. The same color red will display differently on various monitors depending on: the quality of the monitor, the screen resolution, the color depth the monitor is set to, the video card, the amount of video memory, the video processor, and a number of other variables.

Macs and PCs have 256 colors in their system palettes, but only 216 of them are the same colors. The remaining 40 colors vary on Macs and PCs.

You also have to be careful about the hue of a given color. There are pleasant reds and screaming ones. There are warm greens and obnoxious greens. There are strong blues and mellow ones. They will all look different on different monitors and on different systems, but there are safe combinations. The colors used on a Web site need to be combinations that are pleasant to look at and work well together regardless of how the monitor and video card render them. Darker reds are not so emotionally charged and can be a good accent color. And, a large majority of structures have red roofs.

Why should you care about the roof color? Simply put, almost every Web site featuring a bed and breakfast establishment is going to have a photograph of the building (and its roof) on the home page. The colors used to create the Web site **must** interact well with your building's photograph, and often your inn's theme.

Photography and How it Affects Your Message

Few design elements brighten up a Web page more than a well chosen photograph. For that reason, photographs are widely used in building Web pages. They are used to make dramatic home pages, to create buttons, to display products in a catalog, and to create design accents such as borders. Nearly every visually appealing Web site uses photographs in conjunction with other graphics and elements of design like lines and accent colors. The correct photo, in the right spot, sets the tone and conveys the message of the page.

A Web site that presents exceptional photographs sets itself apart by establishing customer appeal and satisfaction.

Conversely, improperly prepared pictures can not only distract from the visual appeal of a Web page but also take so long to download that your visitor will leave. The size of the photographs is the biggest factor in down load time.

Consequently, Web designers prepare their photographs for the Web.

Communication is important in all forms of advertisement, and the Web is no different. Every Web site is trying to sell something. The product or service that is being sold is referred to as the Web site's "offering." (This is true even if you are visiting an educational or informational site – the information becomes the offering..) As a Web designer it is my job to communicate your offering as clearly as possible and as impacting as possible. It is my client's job to furnish me with high quality photographs and other collateral materials necessary to meet their goals.

Managing Photographs on a Web site

Photographs for Web sites must be prepared so that they can be viewed on the Internet. JPEG is the preferred format for photos and other images that require a large color palette.

It is important to accept the fact that color management on the Internet is an inexact science, and it's impossible to generate color consistency on every monitor. Besides the differences between MACs and PCs, the viewer's perception of color can depend on such uncontrollable factors as their ambient light in addition to idiosyncrasies of their computer systems.

Stay Focused

Once you have your logo, your message and your Web address on all your marketing materials – from business cards to stationary, to brochures, to signage, to rack cards, to local advertising, to your Web site, – you can stay focused on what works and increase the effectiveness of your marketing efforts. You'll sleep better at night knowing all your marketing materials are sending a consistent message that will be **Recognized, Received and Remembered!**.

Innkeepers Need Rest and Relaxation

Every innkeeper needs time away from the inn to re-energize. Instead of planning to just get away and play or rest, plan to get away, and continue learning about the industry at the same time.

Educational getaways are a great resource that will keep you connected to the industry and keep you apprised of industry trends while allowing you to visit some outstanding playgrounds. Most state B&B conferences will do that for you. The PAII conferences are always held in interesting and exciting destinations, but keep in mind that the cost to attend a PAII conference is generally much higher than what your state association may charge.

Some of the benefits of annually attending conferences, workshops and seminars include:

- Meet and network with other innkeepers
- Exposure to resources and tools necessary
- Vendors often create special reduced pricing for conference attendees
- The option to watch one or more live demonstration on an innkeeping topic
- Access to training, skill enhancement, professional development and personal growth
- Conferences often include tours of local member inns within a 15 mile radius of the conference location
- Rebuild your enthusiasm
- Keep informed about emerging travel trends
- Door Prizes are often new products -- win so you can try-before-you-buy
- Opportunity to volunteer for projects that will increase overall occupancy
- Fun, Relaxation and Education – all in one place

Chapter Four
The Value of Online Press Release Campaigns

Online media can provide you with the best way to generate business for your inn. News is big business and almost everybody has their favorite programs, news services and publications. Practically every TV program, radio show, magazine and newspaper now has a Web site dedicated to their particular type of topic. Online press releases can get your news posted to these various sites as well as have your releases sent directly to the media outlets in your local area by e-mail.

On Nov 21, 2005 Ken Elliott, owner of the Serenity Bed and Breakfast Inn located in Wichita, Kansas, posted his first online release via the TotalWebDesigner.com online journalism account. Within a few short weeks the release was read by over 25,000 people, picked-up by 561 Internet media outlets, and best of all, the leading local newspaper called him and did their own article featuring his inn. This is just an example of what an online press release can do for a small fee. In this scenario the innkeeper went with the lowest cost release available – at that time just $40 – and he was more than thrilled with the results! Today most Web PR firms charge at least an $80 distribution fee and they go upward from there.

Online Distribution Fees are a Good Value

While higher distribution fees are a bit frightening to some innkeepers, they are often well worth the money. When the Trumpeter Inn, located on the San Juan Island north of Seattle, Washington, was selected as one of the "top places to take your sweetheart" by CNN and Coastal Living in early February of 2006, they not only did an online press release that was eventually read by more than 77,000 people and picked-up by over 900 media outlets. They even paid a distribution fee that included the display of their Web site's home page at the bottom of the release! The response was so overwhelmingly positive, they sent out another release to promote their June Writers' Workshop – it, too, has one of their Web site pages below the release.

And, you don't have to stop with just writing and distributing the release via an online PR firm, you can also place the release on your inn's Web site. Companies post news worthy information on their Web sites all the time. So consider having an Online Press Room page created for your Web site making sure to include contact information so journalists can field their questions to the people qualified to answer.

If you want to avoid phones ringing off the hook from callers who are not journalists or potential guests, use e-mail addresses instead. (I recommend you open one of the free email accounts available on the Internet so you can close the account when the release is out-of-date.) Make it clear that certain numbers or addresses are for media only. Give alternate contacts for other business.

You can get a lot of mileage out of your press releases. Not only are they missiles of information to be shot out to online media outlets, they are informative articles to strengthen your Web site's ranking in search engines. Be careful to make sure they're not just window dressing. Remember to include relevant facts, performance history where appropriate, and contact numbers for the many needs of journalists and potential guests.

Overlooked by many PR professionals, the power of a press release can be extended beyond just traditional media outlets with search engine positioning. Journalists and consumers use the search engines such as Google (www.google.com) and Alta Vista (www.altavista.com) for research. Knowing this, the importance of your press release being found in the top search engines becomes apparent and well worth additional distribution fees.

Search Engine Positioning for Your Press Release

Inclusions/Benefits:

- Submission to the major search engines
- Exposure of your news long after the initial release
- Reach your target audience in a cost effective manner

Creating an Online Release is Easy

All you need to create an online release is pen and paper or a basic computer. Of course, you will also need the contact info for online media distribution company, here are a few of the more popular ones:

- http://www.prnewswire.com
- http://www.prwebdirect.com
- http://www.marketwire.com
- http://emediawire.com

Consider your content as NEWS if:
- Important to general public
- It is timely
- There is human interest
- It is unique or new to the area
- It is on a reporter's desk & nothing else is going on that day

Innkeepers will <u>Almost</u> Always be Submitting "Soft" News

Golden rule when dealing with Media: Always tell the truth!
- Media needs soft news items
  - Inn wins an award
  - Inn donates to a good cause
  - Inn is remodeled
  - Innkeeper performs a community service
  - Innkeeper has Web site redesigned
  - Innkeeper is honored

Writing Press Releases

I know I mentioned earlier that a pen and paper would get you started – and it will. But in today's world, a release to any online media company must be typed and submitted via the company's online template. And, if you purchase distribution that includes photographs, you'll need high resolution photos that tell a story or WOW the reader.

Four "Triggers" of Good Copy:
- Attention
- Interest
- Desire
- Action

Copy Hints
- Headline indicates the content
- You'll need a short Intro
- City and state of origin comes before story
- 1st paragraph "hook" tells the story
- Use short sentences & paragraphs
- Highlight the positives
- Use descriptive language
- Stop at approximately 550 words

Always address the 5 W's and an H
- Who: who is involved
- What: what's happening
- Where: give an exact location
- When: be specific
- Why: why is it happening
- How: heart of the story

Essentials of Good Copy
1. Headline grabs reader's attention.
2. Subhead reinforces the heading.
3. Photo emphasizes the benefit.
4. Body copy starts with a hook.
5. Paragraphs reinforce the benefits.
6. Use everyday language.

7. Proof read, proof read, proof read, and then have someone else proof read one last time!

Writing Copy for the Web

Reading from computer screens is about 25% slower than reading from paper. Even users who are unaware of this research usually say that they feel unpleasant when reading online text. As a result, people don't want to read a lot of text from computer screens: you should write 50% less text. Not just 25% less since it's not only a matter of reading speed but also a matter of feeling good. We also know that users don't like to scroll: one more reason to keep release short. Stop at approximately 550 words.

- Avoid text that repeats photo content
- Fast access is vital ~ site should load in 20 seconds
- People read 25% slower on monitor screens
- Write 50% less text than in print

Include Photographs With Online Press Release

- Photos convey the message of your content
- High quality photos are a MUST
- Select interesting photos with human interest or appeal
- Always include a photo of the exterior of your inn
- When appropriate, include one bedroom view
- Use JPEG format at 300 dpi on photos
- .pdf files are permissible

Common Press Mistakes

Below are some of the most common errors our firm sees on a regular basis. You won't get a second chance to correct the negative impressions left by a poorly written release.

- **All Upper Case Characters** – Never submit a press release in all upper case characters.
- **Grammatical Errors** – Even the best writers occasionally miss grammatical errors and typos. Proof read, Proof read, Proof read. Edit and reproof your press release at least 3 times.
- **Lack of Content** – Make sure you answer the 5 Ws and an H and you'll have substance.
- **Press Releases that Scream BUY ME!** – Do not write your press release like an advertisement. Remember that journalists are NOT your marketing partners. Their job is to relay information to their audience, not to sell. A good press release informs the media.
- **Be Available to Answer Questions** – Never send out a release and then leave town.

Online press releases work and they are an inexpensive way to generate goodwill, keep your business in front of the local public and increase the quality of visitors to your Web site. Having a story appear in online media outlets, your local paper, a trade journal or even a tourism magazine, is akin to an endorsement of you and your B&B.

If you haven't sent out a online press release before, now's the time to get started.

According to information on their Web site, PRWeb.com delivers over 50 million page views of press release content from its sites, PRWeb and eMediaWire. This does not include the traffic they don't measure from their distribution network.

PRWeb also says they "provides roughly 280 categorized feeds over 20,000 corporate feeds. PRWeb was, and may very well be, the only commercial newswire to embrace Yahoo's RSS standard for delivering multimedia content associated with press releases."

One of PRWeb's better features for the $80 and up distribution clients is the placement of the client's home page at the bottom of the online press release! The reader sees the release and as they come to the end of it – bingo – they are on the home page of the Web site.

Another great feature of almost all the online PR distribution operations is the ability to upload large high resolution images that compliment the press release.

This is a terrific service for both the writer of release and the media members. If a newspaper wants to run with a story based on a release, they have instant access to photographs that will print at a high resolution – a must for all newspapers and magazines.

In January of 2006, the Iowa Bed & Breakfast Innkeepers Association was low on registrations for their conference, so an online press release was created and the general public was invited to attend the Aspiring Innkeeper's Boot Camp. The result was 30,400 reads, 628 media pick-ups, increased attendance, and a reporter attended, interviewed and photographed the two main speakers for a story later released.

Dr. B. Marie Brady-Whitcanack was selected as the IBBIA Artist of that year and all the Internet press releases gave additional exposure to her and her unique inn and Art Studio and Gallery.

Dr. B. Marie Brady-Whitcanack can be reached at:
Victoria Bed and Breakfast Inn & Studios
422 Avenue F
Fort Madison, IA 52627
www.victoriabedandbreakfastinnandstudios.com/

Not all your press releases need this much exposure, but when you really want the world to take notice, consider distributing your release online. Utilize the power of the Internet.

Develop a Local Media E-mail List

To contact reporters you need a current media list. The list can include magazines, newspapers, television and radio stations, and state or local bureaus of national wire services such as Associated Press.

If you do not already have such a list, it is time to develop one. You may be able to obtain one from a convention or civic center, or Chamber of Commerce.

The media list should include the names of appropriate reporters and editors. Here is a basic list of the type of editors:

- **Business or Education Editor**
- **Metro and City Desk Editors**
- **Community Events/Calendar Editor**
- **Assignment Editor**
- **Opinions Editor**

Notes:

Chapter Five
A Web site is a MUST HAVE!

The Internet has caused dramatic changes in the lodging industry. As more consumers use the Internet to search for lodging, restaurants, and resorts, innkeepers finding it necessary to step into the learning curve and discover how to harness the immense power of this new phenomenon to improve their bottom line.

In September of 2006, Travelocity.com founder Terry Jones addressed local tourism leaders at the Scottsdale Convention & Visitors Bureau's annual meeting. His address stated that "the Internet has changed forever how people purchase travel, and those who pitch hotels or destinations need to get on board or get left in the low-tech dust. Today's customers are time-starved, tech-savvy and information-rich. By 2009, Americans will be spending $100 billion a year on online travel purchases," Jones said.

"Searching is the second most popular Internet activity, after e-mail," Jones said, with 60 million Americans searching daily for something. "If it's vacation plans, smart [owners] will be at the start of the list of options returned. Figure out what a customer is thinking and give him what he needs."

Innkeepers of the 21st Century must have an online presence. For small business and services, the Internet offers an incredibly cost effective means of advertising. Compared to print, radio and television advertisements, a Web site offers more information together with more possibilities for customer feedback, and accepting reservations.

The Internet removes many of the traditional constraints involved in running a business. Customers no longer have to make a trip to the travel agent to find information and photographs about the vacation destination they've been thinking of visiting.

A well designed bed and breakfast site can be "open" any time your customers have time to shop, allow you to reach a global market and take real-time reservation secured by the guest's credit card.

If your bed and breakfast establishment isn't on the Web, then it's going to lose out to the online competition – it's that simple.

I have found that my best advertising dollar is spent through internet promotion. Whether the guest finds us through a search engine, or calls me for a reservation and can actually go to my site and see the rooms as they make the reservation, a website with a high ranking will assure that we can accommodate the guest that is looking for us.

Liz Norton
Historic Lincoln Hotel
408 Main Street, Box 222
Lowden, IA 52255
www.lincolnhoteliowa.com

Introduction to Domain Names

Simply put, a domain name is a "front" – it is a word sequence that users enter in their browser's location bar to visit a site, but are not a Web site's true address.

Domain names are attached to DNS (Domain Naming System) servers, which are used to translate numeric addresses (known as IP, or Internet Protocol, addresses) into words. Each site you visit on the Internet has a numeric IP address behind its name. This IP is the site's true address on the Web. The domain name is a mask that makes a Web site's true address easier to remember. Here is an example of a domain name: www.totalwebdesigner.com

This domain name has an IP Address of: http:// 64.71.93.174
(The IP is the true web address for www.totalwebdesigner.com)

Domain names are typically categorized by their extension, which is their identifying code. The most popular types of Top Level Domains (TLDs), which are domains that are not associated with a country, are:

.COM: Short for .commercial, and is the most common extension in the world. Many businesses prefer a .com domain name because if offers its name as a recognized status on the internet.

.NET: Short for .network, this domain extension was originally designed to be used by technical Web sites. However, anyone can register this extension.

.ORG: Short for .organization. Originally designated for non-profit firms and any other organization that did not fit under the .com or .net extension. Anyone may now register a .org domain name.

.MUSEUM: This TLD is available only to museums, museum organizations and individual members of the museum profession. More information on the .museum TLD is available at http://musedoma.museum.

.TRAVEL: A new extension for bona fide members of the travel industry. Only pre-authenticated travel related firms, bed and breakfast establishments included, are allowed to purchase a .travel name. Inn travelers can find the consumer's magazine for premier bed and breakfasts inns, "Bed & Breakfast America," at http://www.bba.travel.

.INFO is meant to denote credible information bearing Web sites. It signifies a "resource" Web site. It is the fourth most popular type of web site (the .net, .com, and .org extensions being most popular).

.BIZ is used by small businesses for Web Sites, they tend to be a little bit cheaper than other extensions. A recent poll shows that 97% of attempts to register a .com domain fail. The availability of the new .biz domain presents an opportunity to extend and enhance your company's presence on the web, or just secure the extension with your company name.

.EDU is for schools and other educational sites. It is somewhat restricted and therefore information on these sites are generally given by accredited schools (not diploma mills). Most, if not all colleges, have a .edu website.

.US is for American Web sites and stands for "US". It has more names in inventory than any other extension.

.WS was originally designated as the country code for Western Samoa like .us is for the US, but is now commonly used as an acronym for "Web sites." It is unrestricted and can be registered by anyone, from any country.

.TV is for entertainment entities. Though many are still on the .com (www.vh1.com) extension, some like www.degrassi.tv has TV based content. The .tv website is usually one with rich content or multi-media.

.NAME is the only domain extension specifically designed exclusively for personal use. It is often used to display personal information or pictures.

Selecting a Good Domain Name

You may think it is a brainless task to select a good domain name, but there are a few guidelines you may want to follow.

The first step is selecting a registrar, if you are not going to hire the Web site designer first. (If you think you need to put off actually designing a Web site for a few months, be sure you register and purchase your domain as soon as possible because hundreds, if not thousands, are purchased daily and you won't want to miss an opportunity to purchase just the "right one" for your B&B.)

Selecting a registrar is important, because some of the registrars out there don't allow you to edit your own nameservers or domain preferences. Make sure that you have full administration abilities over your domain names before using any registrar! My personal favorites are Cheap-DomainRegistration.com and GoDaddy.com. Make sure you compare prices when you register your domain name. For instance, it used to cost $70.00 just to register a single domain name through Network Solutions because they held the monopoly. Today there are more competitors, so the price has been driven down to usually between $8.95 and $12.95 per name.

After you've selected your registrar, you need to do a bit of thinking before you actually register a domain name. As you can imagine, most of the good .com domains have been taken, but trust me, there are plenty of good bed and breakfast names left!

Maximizing Your Domain's Potential

Avoid using hyphens: Hyphens make a domain name longer. Although a domain like Bobsinternetresources.com is long, it's not as long as bobs-internet-resources.com. Try describing that URL on the telephone: "It's Bob. hyphen. Internet. hyphen." It can become very cumbersome.

Hyphens No Longer Improve Ranking: There was a time when search engines looked at each word in between hyphens as a keyword. A search engine would then compare each keyword with the content of your site, match it to the query of the user performing the search, and then determine where you site should appear in its listings. Today, however, search engines are much smarter. As a result, hyphenated domain names no longer have any influence on search engine rankings.

Make the Domain Name Memorable: If you can purchase a domain name that is spelled exactly like your inn's name, it is memorable for the guests that have stayed with you in the past, but it is not always possible to buy your inn's exact name. But often you can just add a "bb" or "bedandbreakfast" and be able to purchase a name that will be memorable and contain "keywords" that the search engines will pick up on to determine the theme of your site.

Is .TRAVEL Right for Your B&B?

This new domain name extension is only for bona fide members of the travel industry. Only pre-authenticated travel related firms, bed and breakfast establishments included, will be allowed to purchase a **.travel** domain name. (This can have a great benefit to many inns because it puts them into an elite category.)

While this sounds good initially it does have a few drawbacks. The first is time. It takes much longer to purchase this type of domain name because of the authentication process. The second draw is more critical, because it involves the hosting of your Web site. Not all hosting companies are set-up to host sites with this extension, but GoDaddy.com does host them. (You can't buy a **.travel** domain name from GoDaddy, but they will host it.) And, finally, it is much more expensive to purchase a **.travel** domain name. In December of 2006 one of my clients paid $100 for the first year to register his new **.travel** domain name. I know this will change over time and the fees will lower, but for now these are the realities.

Eligible Domain Names Require Pre-Authentication

There is a rather lengthy process in order to obtain a .travel domain name. Eligible **.travel** names are automatically generated based on the information confirmed in your application, so you will need to complete an online application first and provide supporting documentation for all names for which you seek eligibility.

Also be aware that pre-authentication only assures your eligibility for the requested **.travel** names. Supporting documentation includes but is not limited to:

- A URL that leads to a site using the name that is being requested;
- A name in a URL in any location in the URL is sufficient;
- Anything that a governmental/business authority or customer of the applicant may receive in relation to its business;
- Variations of a used name are acceptable if they are common abbreviations, typo variations or acronyms;
- A name that is proposed for use in a new company or new product/service is acceptable if the applicant documents and provides a business plan to use such a name within 60 days.

Tralliance Corporation Provider is found on the Internet at http://www.authentication.travel/. They register names or you can select from a list of organizations found at http://travel.travel/authproviders.htm to authenticate your **.travel** domain name. Both do business on a first-come, first-served basis and there may be other applicants who are eligible to apply for one or more of the same names, so it is very important to submit your preferred names to the registrar as soon as possible if you feel this new top-level domain may be helpful to your operation – either now or in the future.

A Good Domain Name is Memorable

As you can see, choosing a domain name is not as simple as just thinking up a name. In order for it to be a successful site, you must have a memorable domain name that is both traveler friendly and search engine friendly.

A good domain name usually includes the inn's name. For example: www.hannahmarieinn.com was a perfect choice for the Hannah Marie Country Inn, Spencer, Iowa. It ranks high in search engines, and because it includes the actual name of the inn, it is easy for repeat guests to find on the Internet.

Once your domain name has been purchased, make sure you keep all the important data regarding it in a safe place where you will be able to find it from year to year. Unless you pay for a number of years in advance, you'll need to renew your domain name on an annual basis. It will be necessary to know the name of the company from which it was purchased and its Web site address. Practically all transactions are done via e-mail and live on the Internet in your account accessible control panel.

It is very important for an innkeeper to know who its domain name was purchased from and who is paid to renew it. There are a multitude of scams out there that depend on an innkeeper's lack of knowledge.

I just happened to call the author of this book when she was making a decision on whether or not to include an in-depth discussion on the topic of domain names. The reason I was calling was directly related to the subject she was pondering.

I had received what appeared to be a bill to renew my domain name earlier in the day, but since the rate was twice as high as I had paid in previous years I had wondered if there was a way to tell if it was a legitimate bill. It wasn't real.

Amelia told me how more and more companies sending out fake bills "hoping" a domain name holder will pay them. This practice mimics the former practice of long distance telephone service providers who illegally slammed (stole) customers from one company to enroll the customer elsewhere. Once a domain name owner/registrant makes a payment to one of these companies, it can legally take the domain name over to their registration company. Had I paid that bill, my annual cost for my domain name would have doubled permanently.

Another scam to watch out for is the one where companies attempt to get you to register domain names before someone else does. These scammers depend on the innkeeper's fear. Now, if you want to purchase all the domain names that are similar to yours, fine, there are good reasons to do this. I own several myself, but I bought them all after first discussing each with my Webmaster.

If you are new to innkeeping, be sure you make a point to learn about all the various scams that keep coming back around every year. There are a number of e-mail scams that have caused innkeepers lost revenue, so investigate and learn how to recognize them or you too may end-up victimized by one in the future. The scammers are clever and they are not just here in the US, they are working their bunko tactics all over the globe.

Esther Kauffeld-Hoffa
Garden and Galley B&B
1321 S. Jefferson Way
Indianola, IA 50125
www.gardenandgalley.com

Design and Performance Online Does Matter

The Internet is loaded with poorly designed sites that fail to perform well in search engines. If a Web site isn't pleasant to view and navigate, the visitor will leave. If a site is not designed to perform well in search engines, no one will ever find it without the exact Web address. This type of Web site is a complete failure.

While HTML (the basic code used to create a Web site) is relatively easy to learn, design is an art form that cannot be mastered so quickly. Colour theory, balance and layout are just some aspects of design. Added to that are a multitude of industry standards and the practical necessities of keeping download time low. (This ensures the site is visible to a maximum number of people.)

Problems often connected to poorly designed Web sites, include:

- **Incorrect spelling.** Nothing interrupts the flow of text quite like a "misspelt" word.
- **Garishly clashing colors.** You don't need to have an art degree to realize that bright red on bright green is not a pleasant combination.
- **Blinking text.** Most flashing graphics and animated characters zooming across the pages are distracting. These effects are not impressive; they're annoying and

distracting to visitors that desire to calmly and seriously consider staying at your lodging establishment..

- **Haphazard navigation.** Your visitors should be able to concentrate on the content of your site, view the bedrooms easily and not have to search for a button to learn how to make a reservation.
- **Minuscule text.** This is hard to read and very frustrating to the visitor who seriously wants to do business with you.
- **Giant text.** This is equally hard to read
- **Huge graphics.** These will increase download time and encourage visitors to leave before the graphics are finished downloading. You want to have good sized photos of your rooms on your site, but these images should not take-up the entire page or be of such a large file size that it takes more than 20 seconds to load.
- **"Now Under Construction" notices.** Don't allow your designer to have these pages live on the Internet. If the page is not ready, it should not be online. It's that simple!
- **Music on a lodging site.** Studies have shown that many employees search for vacation and get-away information while at their desks at work. (Many search during their lunch hour.) Few office environments want employee's work computer blasting music.

A hospitality/lodging Web site should always be on the cutting edge and incorporate some, if not all of the following:

* Sophisticated designs using the latest design tools and techniques

* Flash animation and/or a virtual tour

* Professional look and feel with an emphasis on usability and easy navigation

* Dynamic, database-driven news blog on which the innkeeper can post current events, testimonials, press releases and lodging packages on

* Advanced search capabilities in the blog

* High quality fast loading images of the rooms and property

* Contact and Request for Information

*Real-time Online Availability/Reservation capabilities

A Web site Developer With Lodging Experience is Best

Select your designer carefully and be sure he or she has extensive background in creating lodging and/or tourism related Web sites. Price is not the most important factor when selecting a Web design firm to work with.

Don't Spend Much on Web Hosting

If you are a small inn that is just beginning to define your online presence, you don't need a whole lot of bells and whistles when it comes to Web site hosting.

You most certainly don't need 10,000MB (10GB) of web space and 100,000MB (100GB) of bandwidth each month. So don't pay for it! You might be thinking, "Well, if it's relatively cheap and I may need it in the future, why don't I just order it now?" That kind of reasoning paves the road to overspending.

Your Web Developer Can Live Anywhere

Many developers work virtually, that is, directly through the Internet and via e-mail. It would not be uncommon to never have in-person contact. This 21ˢᵗ Century style of work is very different than the conventional. The lack of face-to-face contact makes it easy for both parties to simply forget about the project as time goes on. You need to take steps to ensure your project won't stagnate. Agree on a solid timeline with clear milestones, expectations, and deadlines so that it is easy for both you and the developer to stay on target.

Quickly Provide Designer with Feedback

Although you are paying a design firm for its creativity and industry knowledge, remember, you make the final decisions.

Working with a Web designer is a step-by-step, layer-by-layer process. If you don't respond with feedback immediately, your designer may have already completed other layers of the site before your feedback reaches them. This means they must not only re-work the layer in question, but also the following layers. Some designers have been "abused" so many times in this manner they will just wait patiently for your feedback before they go on to the next layer of work.

When we decided to move a historical building on our business property and restore it as a bed and breakfast inn, we knew that we'd need to work with a designer that takes clients though a sequential process that begins with an analysis of an inn's objectives and target market. We also knew the information gathered from this process would help our designer complete a Web site unique to our business.

We gave our designer ideas of what we thought we wanted, asked questions, and supplied her with links to sites with features close to what we wanted to end-up with. We prepared drafts of the text we wanted on the site and gave her a list of all the keywords we felt were important to our business.

As the final design came to life, we went over the edits and changes we desired regarding layout, color scheme, navigation method and theme. In the end, we had the beginning of a Web site that will continue to evolve over the course of the next year as we complete the restoration work on our new lodging facility, and open for guests in November of 2007.

Since we have been working with a designer experienced in the lodging industry, our new site functions well in the search engines and has brought us telephone inquiries months before we were ready to take reservations. By the time we opened for business we had already built a strong foundation for success on and off the Internet.

Donna Muilenburg
Okoboji Country Inn
1712 Terrace Park Blvd
Milford, IA 51331
www.okobojicountryinn.com

Domain Ownership

The most common mistake domain owners make is allowing incorrect contact information in their domain's WHOIS record, which essentially serves as a domain's record of ownership.

WHOIS is a directory of domain name information. When you register a domain name, your postal address, e-mail address and phone number are automatically published in the public WHOIS database. The Internet Corporation for Assigned Names and Numbers (ICANN), the nonprofit body responsible for accrediting domain name registrars, requires that this personal information be accurate and available for anybody to view on the Internet. There are a number of WHOIS resources on the Internet, but this is a straight-forward resource that is not attempting – today anyway – to sell you anything: http://www.who.is/

There are several components to a WHOIS record, all or most of which is completed when registering a domain name. These components include the following:

Registrant: The person or organization that registered the domain name and legally owns it. Let me emphasize again -- the **registrant** is the person that **legally owns** the domain name.

Administrative Contact: The person or organization responsible for all administrative issues pertaining to the domain name, including registrant information. This is one of the most important aspects of your registration record. If your e-mail address or the e-mail address of someone you trust

100% is not listed, you essentially have no control over the domain name.

Billing Contact: This is the person or organization responsible for handling any billing issues related to the domain name.

Technical Contact: The technical contact is the person or organization that should be contacted regarding any technical issues pertaining to your domain. This is the category that would have your Webmaster's name and contact information.

If you ever wish to sell, transfer or otherwise modify your domain in a significant manner, there is a good chance your Administrative Contact will have to become involved. As a result, it is absolutely crucial that your contact information remain up to date – otherwise, making any adjustments to your domain will become frustrating, and potentially impossible.

Notes:

Glossary of Domain Name Terms

Domain servers: This contains the DNS (Domain Name System) information for a domain, and is usually listed in WHOIS records. There are usually two lines of DNS information. The first is typically a site's primary DNS information, while the second contains secondary/back-up information.

DNS: Short for Domain Name System which is used to translate numeric addresses (known as IP, or Internet Protocol, addresses) into words.

Domain name: the word sequences users enter to visit a site.

HTTP: Stands for HyperText Transfer Protocol, the protocol by which HTML files move across the Internet. HTTP requires a client browser and an HTTP server (typically a Web server).

ICANN: Stands for Internet Corporation for Assigned Names and Numbers, which is a not for profit organization that handles IP address space allocation and most other regulatory tasks associated with domain names.

IP Address: The numeric address behind a domain name that holds a website's real location on the Web.

Propagation or Migration: The process where name servers throughout the Internet add new domains and remove expired ones from their records. This can be a lengthy process, which is why connecting to a new domain name can often take three or four days.

SSL: Short for Secure Sockets Layer, a protocol developed by Netscape to handle and protect confidential/sensitive information required for e-commerce transactions (like credit card numbers). SSL address usually begin with 'https'. Never give out your credit card info online unless you see the https:// at the beginning of the address line.

WHOIS: A central database which tracks all domain name/IP registrations. Each domain name registrar typically maintains its own version of a WHOIS database.

Chapter Six

How to Achieve Higher Search Engine Rankings

A top position on a major search engine can increase traffic to your inn's Web site. Web site visitors are usually potential guests seeking lodging in your area or community.

A Web designer specializing in the Bed & Breakfast Industry has daily discussions with innkeepers and knows how to obtain top ranking positions on a major search engine.

The Internet has changed the marketing mix for Bed and Breakfast inns – as much as 91% of all new business will come from the Internet in 2008. And, inns can now take reservations directly from their Web site – this was unheard of just a few short years ago.

You'll need a general understanding of how people use the Internet, what search engines are, where they come from, and how they work. Let's first learn some important search engine key terms.

Internet Spider or Robot: A "software spider" is an unmanned program operated by a search engine that surfs the Web. The spider reads and indexes the entire text of each Web site it visits into the main database of the search engine it is working for. (Images, drawings and photographs are not indexed – only text.) What the spider finds on your site will determine how your site is indexed. Search engines determine a site's relevancy based on a complex scoring system that most search engines keep secret. This formula adds or subtracts points based on things like how many times the keyword appeared on the page, where on the page it appeared, and how many total words were found. The pages that achieve the most points are ranked at the top of the search results, the rest are buried at the bottom, never to be found.

Crawling: A term for a search engine that is actively searching the Web for more content. Most engines allow you to submit your site for a scheduled visit.

Directory: A categorical listing of sites available on the World Wide Web. Directories are compiled by humans, not by search engines.

Internet: A worldwide network of computer networks, sometimes referred to as "the Net." Notice the word is always capitalized.

WWW (World Wide Web): a *part* of the Internet designed to allow easier navigation of the network through the use of graphical user interfaces and hypertext links between different addresses The World Wide Web is the most commonly used application on the Internet. It is sometimes referred to as "the Web" – make a note, the word is capitalized.

Primary Search Results: Results that are initially displayed after a search has been performed at a search engine or a directory.

Paid search results: Search results that are paid for by an advertiser. Paid search results are usually displayed at the top of the page, along the right hand side of the page or at the beginning along with the primary search results.

Audience Reach Percentage (ARP): The percentage of the entire Internet audience reached by a particular search engine or directory over a 30-day period. An ARP of 1 percent would indicate that 1 percent of the total Internet audience utilized the search site at least once within the last 30 days.

Algorithm: A set of rules that a search engine uses to rank the listings contained within its index, in response to a particular query.

Uniform Resource Locator (URL): Put simply, it is a Web address! URL is also referred to as a Universal Resource Locator, but it still refers to a "Web address."

Here is a URL: www.totalwebdesigner.com.

A Little History

Have you ever wondered what the difference is between the Internet and the World Wide Web? Many people mistakenly believe that the two terms can be used interchangeably. In actuality, nothing could be further from the truth.

The Internet is a worldwide network of computer networks. It was conceived in 1969 by a U.S. government agency called the Advanced Research Projects Agency(ARPA). There are several applications commonly used on the Internet today, including e-mail and the World Wide Web. We'll look at a few examples.

E-mail address: amelia@totalwebdesigner.com

World Wide Web Address (or URL):
http://www.totalwebdesigner.com

File Transfer Protocol Address (this is one way to access a server): ftp.totalwebdesigner.com

The World Wide Web is, by far, the most commonly used application on the Internet. All users of the Web utilize HTTP, or the hypertext transfer protocol. Look at the address bar near the top of your Web browser. You'll find that the **www** is preceded by **http://**. This tells the Web site that you're visiting on the World Wide Web and that you're using the hypertext transfer protocol.

Understanding the difference between the Internet and the World Wide Web is important. While search engines utilize the Internet, they do not search the entire Internet. Search engines only search for Web sites on the World Wide Web. Why? Because search engines are automated. Once search engine programs are written, they can run and compile detailed indexes of Web sites without any human intervention whatsoever.

Although it is said they "crawl" or "spider" the Web in their hunt for pages to include in their database, in truth they stay in one place. They find the pages for potential inclusion by following the links in the pages they already have in their database. They cannot think or type a Web address or use judgment to "decide" to go look something up and see what's on the Web about it. (Computers are getting more sophisticated all the time, but they are still brainless.)

If a Web page is never linked to any other page, search engine spiders cannot find it. The only way a brand new page -- one that no other page has ever linked to -- can get into a search engine is for its Web address to be submitted by some human to the search engine companies as a request that the new page be included. All search engine companies offer ways to do this.

Because search engine companies are constantly changing, being bought, and being sold, it's important to keep tabs on which search engines are being used the most. One of the better resources I've found is *"Search Engine Watch,"* visit them online at www.searchenginewatch.com.

Web Directories

What is a Web Directory? A web directory is a collection of links broken down into relevant categories. Think Yahoo! and their directory, the Open Directory Project (ODP) or even the Google Directory (which is pulled from the ODP). At its most basic level, a Web directory is a collection of links made available to the public.

Yahoo! was started as a directory, not a search engine. Yahoo! and Google are the most popular Directories on the Internet. While search engines' indexes are compiled by computers, directories are categorical lists of Web sites that are compiled by humans. Each web site that is listed in a directory has been carefully scrutinized and deemed acceptable for placement in one specific category.

Yahoo! was founded in February 1994 by David Filo and Jerry Yang. Yahoo! is actually an acronym for *Yet Another Hierarchical Officious Oracle*. Yahoo! was incorporated in 1995 with an initial investment of almost $2 million.

In an effort to diversify, Yahoo! early on decided to utilize Google's engine to supply users with primary search results. However, in February of 2004, Yahoo! unveiled its own brand new search engine. Yahoo!'s directory can still be tapped into and is extremely useful when searching for information on the Web. To retrieve Yahoo!'s directory results, you must first perform a regular search at Yahoo! When the results page appears, simply click the **Directory** link, and the directory results will instantaneously appear.

Benefits of Being Listed in a Web Directory

In theory, there are two main benefits of being listed in a Web directory: Increased link-popularity and increased Web traffic. As far as link-popularity is concerned, you need to factor in several variables:

- The Page Rank of the directory

- The Page Rank of the category page on which you are listed
- Where you are listed on the page
- The number of competing sites on that page

Yahoo! and Open Directory Project are the two biggest directories on the Internet, these are the main two we'll discuss.

- **Yahoo!** A listing in Yahoo!'s directory has direct benefits: Google – and other search engines as well – give your website an added importance if your website is listed in the Yahoo! directory.
- **The Open Directory Project (ODP)** The open directory project is a directory that rivals the reach of Yahoo! Why? Because directories like the Google Directory and many others are powered by its results. This gives a listing in the ODP a very high premium. However, because a listing in ODP is essentially free, there is very little you can do about the time its takes to be indexed. Many sites that are submitted are never indexed. On the other hand, quality Web sites that are added into their relevant categories are almost always accepted. It is important to understand that the ODP lists a high proportion of informational and non-profit sites – due to the fact that human volunteers are approving and disallowing all submissions..

If you do not find your inn's Web site listed on the OPD, you can submit it yourself. It is <u>critical that you follow their submission guidelines</u>. The OPD hierarchical directories are complicated, so make sure you do a little surfing in the OPD prior to attempting to submit your Web site. Complete instructions for submitting to the Open Directory Project are found at: http://www.dmoz.org/add.html.

Take your time and a serious look prior to attempting to submit your site.

The Open Directory Project is compiled by more than 75,000 volunteers who have indexed nearly 4 million Web sites. The directory contains just under 500,000 categories, all of which can be searched by keyword or by category.

Top 2 Power Engines

Today, two search engines and directories receive more than 81.1% percent of all search traffic. The two are:

Google

http://www.google.com

Google's primary search results come from its spider-based index. It also houses a search tool that allows users to search for images on the Web. Google is able to search UseNet newsgroups, as well. Google is also capable of displaying directory results, which are provided, in part, by the Open Directory Project.

Google provides primary search results to AOL Search, iWon Search, and Go.com. The engine also provides paid search results to AOL Search, Teoma, Netscape, iWon Search, Ask Jeeves, and Go.com, yet less than half the searchable Web is fully searchable in Google.

Google is the most difficult to obtain high rankings at because the company guards its ranking formula (**algorithm**) so closely. The creators of search engines change the way they calculate relevance and guard their methodology; being high in the major search engines' rankings on a topic means big business. If a site has high PageRank, it is spidered more often and more deeply. There is no perfect way to ensure that you'll receive a high ranking.

Even if you do get a great ranking, there's no assurance that you'll keep it for long. Knowledge is your best tool when playing the search engine ranking game.

Yahoo!

http://www.yahoo.com

While it is clear that Google has overtaken Yahoo! in popularity – for now – the race is far from over. The technology of "search" remains in its infancy. Obtain high rankings on Yahoo! by following their guidelines to higher ranking. They are not real detailed, but they are helpful, you'll find them at this Web address:

http://help.yahoo.com/help/us/ysearch/ranking/ranking-02.html

Here is a search engine submission tip: Before submitting to any directory, take the time to prepare a 25 word or less description of your entire web site. This description should make use of the two or three most important key terms (Example: Fostoria, Iowa, bed and breakfast)

Algorithms Used by Spiders

An algorithm is a mathematical formula used by search engine spiders to rank and position web sites in their database/indexes. A spider/robot/crawler is a software program that automatically retrieves web pages. Spiders are used to feed pages to search engines. I'm not sure who initially began calling this process "spidering," but it makes sense because the software "crawls" across the Web.

Because most Web pages contain links to other pages, a spider can start almost anywhere. As soon as it sees a link to another page, it goes off and fetches/retrieves it. If the links are hidden on a site in a Flash movie or in javascript coding, the spiders will be unable to index. Spiders can't see anything in javascript, graphical elements (photos, drawings or illustrations) or Flash. Web designers can overcome this limitation by using what is known as ALT text as they insert images onto a page. (You can generally view ALT text by placing your mouse on top of an image. The ALT text will appear in a second or two.)

Before a search engine can serve results to Web surfers, it must have a database that it can search. As a spider crawls the Web, it indexes, or logs, each Web site it visits. The log is saved as an entry in the search engine's database. Each entry includes the Web address, and important keyword information.

When you initiate a search at a search engine, the engine is not actively searching the Web for the keywords that you provide it. It's searching the entire database, or index, that it has compiled from its most recent crawl.

When writing content (copywriting) for a Web page, it is important to remember to write for the visitor as well as the search engine spider.

For a decent search engine ranking, you should try to have approximately 200 - 250 words of text on every page of your site, with a few keywords and phrases strategically thrown into the content so the spiders can index your pages accurately.

Don't use a great deal of marketing babble or romantic verses. Keep the content rich, concise and focused. Be sure to include a few relevant keywords and keyphrases here and there without making the content confusing for the visitor.

Hash Tables

Search engines use indexes so that users can get results as quickly as possible. Typically, a hash table is used to create the index. The hash table uses a formula to assign numerical values to words. The numerical values are then distributed evenly into a set number of divisions. The values are then searched for, instead of the words. Let me demonstrate why this is helpful.

Let's say a Web surfer named Esther is searching for the word accommodation. Another Web surfer named Mary is searching for the word quaint. If search engines didn't use hash tables, Esther would get her search results much faster than Mary. This is because the word accommodation starts with the letter A, and the word quaint starts with the letter Q. Since many more words in the English language begin with the letter A than the letter Q, Mary's search would take much longer. Simply put, hash tables make it possible for both searches to achieve results at the same speed.

But how does a search engine know that your Web site exists? There are two primary ways that search engines index Web sites:

1.   The Web site is submitted to the search engine database.
2.   Another Web site that has been indexed has linked to the Web site.

How often a search engine performs a complete crawl varies from spider to spider. Google, the current search engine leader, performs a complete crawl roughly every six to eight weeks. However, it updates its index of **already-databased** sites more frequently.

When a site is indexed by a search engine, it runs through a complex algorithm (formula) that determines the site's search engine ranking. Each search engine algorithm is unique, and the actual algorithms are not public knowledge. Search engines are constantly updating and changing their algorithms. This serves two purposes:

1. Constantly modifying the algorithm allows search engine companies to constantly improve the relevancy of their search results.

2. By constantly changing the algorithm, a search engine company can prevent their exact algorithm from becoming public knowledge. There are thousands of search engine experts and Webmasters always trying to determine search engine algorithms. Even the most complex algorithm would eventually be determined if it were left unchanged.

It is always a challenge, as a Web designer, to move a new Web site upward in search engine rankings because on any given day thousands of new sites are being added to the Internet.

One of the ways my company's creative team gets new sites indexed and listed on the top search engines quickly is by placing a link to the new site in a high quality existing site – like our own. Adding a link to the new site on one of our popular pages that is visited regularly by the search engines expedites the indexing process and often pushes the new site upward in ranking.

The more high quality links a new site can having pointing to it, the faster the new site will move upward into the top ranking positions on the most popular search engines.

All of the major search engines and directories strive to provide the best search experience on the Web by directing searchers to high-quality and relevant web content in response to any search query. Unfortunately for all of us, there are many pages created deliberately to trick the search engine into offering inappropriate, redundant or poor-quality search results. These pages are often referred to as "spam." None of the engines want these pages in their index, so they go to great lengths to keep them out. From time to time, this practice could actually keep a meaningful Web site out – one of the reasons you want a skilled professional, with experience in the hospitality industry, creating your Web site.

Search Engine Optimization (SEO)

The art of search engine optimization or SEO is the process of increasing the number of visitors to a Web site by obtaining a high ranking in the search results of a search engine.

Search engines are the key to finding specific information on the vast expanse of the World Wide Web. The higher the Web site ranks, the more likely it is to be visited. A high ranking is essential as the majority of search engine visitors generally only look at the first page or two of the search results.

When a Web site is especially developed with search engines rankings in mind, this is known as search engine optimization. Over 80% of Internet traffic is generated by search engines. According to a press release from the Computer Industry Almanac Inc on November 14, 2005, the worldwide number of Internet broadband subscribers will surpass 215 million in 2005—up from less than 5M in 1999 and 67M in 2002. The Internet can be a limitless resource of potential customers for your business.

The basics of SEO must be used by your Web designer or your site is doomed to be lost in cyberspace and only found by those who have the exact URL (Web address) or stumble across it by accident.

If you are going to hire a Web designer, be sure they understand the hospitality industry. Even the selection of your domain name will play a part in your site's rankings in the search engines.

Your Web designer, if knowledgeable about the hospitality industry, will create a list of keywords that he or she feels is relevant to the Web site. The list should include single words and keyword phrases. Because a designer that specializes in lodging reads server logs and site visitor reports regularly, they will know which keywords and keyword phrases are used by most searchers to find lodging. They will also know which keywords are most often spelling incorrectly – this is important because those keywords can be listed in the source code for the Web page as a keyword Meta Tag.

To look at the source code for any Web page, follow these instructions: For Internet Explorer, click the **View** menu, then click **Source Code**. The source code will immediately appear in Notepad. If you're using Netscape Navigator, click the **View** menu, then click **Page Source**. The source code will appear in Netscape's code viewer.

Meta Tags

Before we can talk about Meta Tags, it helps to know just a little about the source code that creates a Web page. HyperText Markup Language (HTML) is a computer coding language used to make hypertext documents for use on the Web. HTML resembles old-fashioned typesetting code, where a block of text is surrounded by codes that indicate how it should appear. HTML allows text to be "linked" to another file or page on the Internet.

Using Meta Tags in the HTML source code allows the Web designer to have a certain amount of control over how a site is indexed. (They are not cure-alls, but will give your site the edge in most cases.) Many search engines no longer use them for indexing, but some still do. And, since algorithms of the major search engines are so closely guarded, it is better to be on the safe side and use Meta Tags because your site will not be punished, and my experience as a Web designer supports their use.

There is an excellent chart online about Search Engine Ranking Factors (The document and page were created Oct 06, 2005), here is the link:

http://www.seomoz.org/articles/search-ranking-factors.php#2

On the chart you'll find the following info, along with much more:

- Although largely a remnant of the early days of web markup, the meta keywords tag is still used by search engines as a reference point for the terms targeted by the page. It can be of value to place common misspellings of your primary targets, if any, into this tag.

- **The meta description tag is almost completely outdated in markup, but is still useful for describing your page accurately to search engines.** In some cases, the engines may even use this tag as the description of your site in the results page listings. Many professionals question the value of this tag. I'm not at all sure if has any affect on ranking, but I use it just in case.

- Using the keyword term/phrase in the actual URL of the document may be assigned some weight by search engines, whether used in hyphenation or strung together.

- Search engine may consider the value of a keyword or related term/phrase in the actual domain name of the site. Relevant terms/phrases would thereby benefit sites with those terms/phrases in their name.

Few innkeepers design their own Web sites so learning HTML coding is not necessary. But, I do encourage innkeepers to understand how to identify Meta Tags so they can be certain their designer uses them in the source code.

The text in the title tag is crucial in letting search engines know what each page is about. Here is an example of a title tag:

<title>Spencer Iowa Bed and Breakfast - Hannah Marie Country Inn</title>

The other tags are not as important as the title tag, but the description tag is still used by some search engines. Here is what the description tag looks like:

<META name="description" content="a description of your page">

Depending on the search engine, this will be displayed along with the title of your page in an index. The tag "content" could be a word, sentence or even paragraph to describe your page. Keep this tag reasonably short, concise and to the point - most importantly: accurate!

The third most important tag is a 'keyword' or 'keyword phrase' tag. A keyword or keyword phrase is a word or combination of words that people type into search engines to find what they are looking for. It is important to use the keyword phrase in the meta title and throughout the page where it makes sense, as well as in the meta description. Here is what a keyword tag looks like:

<META name="keywords" content="a, list, of, keywords">

Choose whatever keywords you think are appropriate, separated by commas. Remember to include synonyms, Americanisms, and words you know are often misspelled. It is best to separate keywords with a coma. A space after the coma is not necessary.

(Example: Iowa Bed and Breakfasts,ia,iowa,IA,Iowa,bed and breakfast,bandb,inn,inns,lodging,B&B,accommodations,bed& breakfast,luxury lodging,farm stay,country inn, etc.)

Here is an example of well-written Meta Tags:

```
<html>
<head>

<TITLE>Indianola Iowa Bed and Breakfast - Garden and
Galley B&B Inn – Indianola Iowa Lodging
Accommodations</TITLE>

<META name="description" content="Indianola Iowa Bed and
Breakfast Accommodations - Garden & Galley B&B offers
romantic lodging accommodations. ">

<META name="keywords" content="Indianola Iowa Bed and
Breakfast, indianola, ia, lodging, iowa bed and breakfast,
indianola iowa lodging, iowa, b&amp;b, b and b, iowa inn,
guest accommodation, accomodation,
accommodations,inns,indianola B&B,Indianola lodging">

</head>
```

As you can see, the **keyphrase** for this site is: Indianola
Iowa Bed and Breakfast. This phrase is much more important
in the source code than the name of the establishment.

When looking at the source code, examine the page title.
Check to see if your inn's keyphrase is found within the title.
Also, take a look at the page description and the keyword list.
If the keyphrase is missing, you need to take steps to have it
inserted.

If there are any keywords found within the page that you feel are appropriate to the content of your Web site, add them to your keyword list.

When determining which keywords you'd like to include within your HTML documents, you'll need to make sure that the words you choose aren't trademarked. For example, let's say you include the word *Pepsi* in your keyword list. Technically, the Pepsi Cola Company could sue you for damages, especially if your Web site gets ranked in a higher position than theirs.

The number of keyword-related lawsuits is growing, and more companies are jumping on the bandwagon every day. In most cases, common sense dictates what is acceptable and what is unacceptable. For example, if your last name is Pepsi, you could most likely get away with having *Pepsi* in your keyword list (that is, if your Web site has to do with you or your family).

You can be sued for content in your Meta Tags. Danny Sullivan, editor of Searchenginewatch.com has listed a few of the lawsuits in this context and precautions one needs to take. Here is a link to his article:

http://searchenginewatch.com/resources/article.php/2156551

One example Sullivan reviews involved Playboy. Playboy sued two adult web site operators who spammed their pages with the word Playboy and Playmate hundreds of times. This helped them rise to the top of some search engine results for a search on "Playboy." The defendants were also using the terms Playboy and Playmate in the site names, the domain names and in their slogans.

A San Francisco federal judge issued a preliminary injunction against the operators, deciding that trademark infringement and false representation could be proven at trial.

Keyword Effectiveness

The Meta Keywords Tag includes keywords that tell search engines about the content of your Web site. The more important the keyword, the sooner it should be presented within the keyword list.

Where you place your keywords are critical. For example, in most search engines, placing the keywords in the title tag of the page will give it relevancy. On some engines, placing keywords in the link text (the part that is underlined on the screen in a browser) can add relevancy to those words.

Always remember, each search engine has their own formula for determining where your site will rank when a visitor completes a search.

Generally, each search engine's algorithm assigns "points" to Web sites in their database. And, while all search engines measure a keyword's position on your pages, there are a variety of places where you can include keyword-rich copy. Right now, we are simply talking about basic keyword placement and general rules you should consider when working with a designer to create site descriptions and titles for your pages.

While the ranking criteria vary among search engines, most grade the placement of keywords on your Web site, the site's title and description based on these factors:

1. Keyword Prominence
2. Keyword Frequency
3. Site Popularity
4. Keyword Weight
5. Keyword Proximity
6. Keyword Placement

You don't want to let the designer go overboard with frequency. Some search engines will punish your site if a word or phrase is repeated too many times – the site will be penalized for "spamming" or what is called "keyword stuffing" in the design world.

Site popularity is based on the number of other **relevant** Web sites linked to your site. This ranking measurement is one you as an innkeeper have some control over. You can contact your local Chamber office, destination attractions in the area, and business networking groups in the tourism community and ask them to place a link to your inn's Web site on their site.

Search engines prefer to find links from authoritative sites, or links from sites that share the same focus as your site – having all your relatives point their family history Web site or a used car lot site to your B&B site could actually work against you in the long run. These are not the type of links you want pointing to your bed and breakfast site.

Stay within the travel, hospitality and tourism industries when requesting another Web site to point to yours.

Google's Algorithm – A Helpful Chart

I'm going to share a chart with you that a fellow Web designer put together after doing some in-depth research on the Google Algorithm.

Is this chart accurate? Who knows, the designer doesn't work for Google and doesn't know anyone who does that will share this closely guarded secret, but she has been studying the Google Algorithm for a number of years and is very good at getting all the Web sites she designs in the top 5 positions on Google. Everyone on my creative team keeps this chart near their desk just for a quick reminder.

I'm sharing it because it will give you, as an innkeeper, a guideline to following as your work with your Web designer.

Google Algorithm

Topic	Importance
Link Popularity	25%
Title	25%
URL & File Name	10%
Heading Text	10%
Body Content	20%
Images ALT text	10%
Total	100%

Link Popularity

Because link popularity is so important, I've decided to list what other professionals have to say about this topic:

> "Search for sites that rank high for search terms that are important to you [yoursite], then look through the search results for sites that do not compete with you. These sites should be high on your list of link targets. Piggy back on their high ranking." *(Eric Ward, President,* NetPOST and URLwire)

> "Think in terms of related fields as opposed to actual competition. Are there any organizations or associations connected with your industry? What about educational establishments? Publications? News sites?" *(Robin Nobles of the Academy of Web Specialists and Search Engine Workshops)*

> "Link quality simply means how well positioned the pages are that link to you. A high quality link is in one of the top five positions on page one of the search engine being use. (As a designer I want my client's sites to be in one of the top five positions on the three most popular search engines. As of the writing of this book the top three would be Google, Yahoo! and MSN,

but remember, this is always subject to change! ~ *Amelia Painter*)

There are also boosts and penalties involved. If you are linked to by a spammy link farm, you get a penalty. If you are linked to by a directory like Yahoo! or LookSmart.com you get a boost. What about the hundreds of free directories? Every relevant link helps.' *(~ Michael Campbell with Internet Marketing Secrets)*

Keyword Density

Keyword density is another critical element for high search engine ranking. Keyword density is specified as a percentage. Keyword density needs to be balanced correctly (too low and you will not get the optimum benefit, too high and your page might get flagged for "keyword spamming").

Keyword Density is the number of times a specific keyword or keyphrase appears in your HTML document, divided by the total number of words in the HTML document.

Here's the formula described mathematically:

$$KD = N/T$$

KD = Keyword density
N = Number of times the keyword appears in the HTML document
T = Total number of words in the HTML document

For example, let's say we've optimized a Web page for the keyphrase "iowa bed and breakfast." Let's say the designer used this keyphrase four times in your entire HTML document, which contains a total of 100 words. Here's how these numbers would fit into the formula:

$$KD = 4/100$$
$$KD = .04$$
$$(.04 = 4\%)$$

So, our keyword density is equal to 4 percent.

Experts always seem to debate the best keyword density for the highest possible rankings. Our company and most of the designers I chat with regularly believe a keyword density of 1 percent to 7 percent for the entire HTML document is optimal. Most agree that overall a site should attempt to attain a keyword density of 3 percent to do well in the 12 major search engines.

The Web Site has provided immediate information about not only our historic bed and breakfast and art workshops, but, also details regional sites of interest to tourists, making the bed and breakfast and Fort Madison a destination site.

Dr. B. Marie Brady-Whitcanack
Victoria Bed and Breakfast Inn & Studios
422 Avenue F
Fort Madison, IA 52627
www.victoriabedandbreakfastinnandstudios.com/

Below is a formula I picked-up while taking a University class on the subject of search engine optimization:

Page Title: 5%-10% Goal
META Description: 5%-10% Goal
META Keyword List: 5%-10% Goal
Visible Text: 1%-2% Goal
Total Overall: 3% Goal

If your Web site designer aims for these keyword density percentages, without spamming keywords, your Web site rankings will be dramatically increased.

Submitting Your Site to Search Engines

As an innkeeper I'm sure you won't feel you have the time to be submitting your Web site to the 12 major search engines, especially since most Web design firms include an initial submit with their fee.

The important word in the sentence above is "initial" or one time. Unless you pay for Internet Marketing, the designer is finished with his or her submission obligation once the initial submit is completed. I recommend you take the time, on a regular basis, to submit your site to every search engine you can find. New search engines are always popping-up, and who knows if it will be a huge success or a big flop, so don't be hesitant about listing your site.

Online Lodging Directories

There are now hundreds of lodging directories to invest advertising dollars. Destination directories and travel resources are frequently visited by potential guests searching for lodging.

The more of these lodging directories listing your inn, the better chance you have of getting your selling message to the guest that is seeking lodging in your area.

It is extremely important that you list your property in as many of the free ones you can find, but also invest in a few of the subscription-based directories. (We'll talk about this in a moment.)

The top online directories are a good return on investment dollars, but innkeepers **should not** purchase listings at online directories unless they include a link that will take guests directly to their personal Web sites.

Top directories are subject to change rapidly on the Internet, innkeepers need to learn how to determine exactly which directories will bring them the best return on investment. One way to make this determination is to type in the name of your city, state and the words "bed and breakfast" on Google or Yahoo!. Then, see which lodging directories rank the highest for your geographic area.

For the past three years **www.bedandbreakfast.com** has been the most popular B&B Directory on the Internet followed closely by www.bbonline.com. But, we are talking about the Internet, an environment subject to rapid change, so use the simple formula I gave you above.

It's important, so let me repeat the formula for finding a lodging directory ranked highest for your geographic area:

> **Type in the name of your city, state and the words "bed and breakfast" on Google or Yahoo!. Then, see which lodging directories rank the highest for your geographic area.**

Calculating Return on Investment for Online Directory

Most online B&B Directories change an annual fee to be listed and have a link back to your inn's Web site. This means at least once a year you must make a decision as to which Directory or Directories you will subscribe. Will you renew or do some search engine research to find out which B&B Directory is marketing heavily in your community and give them a try?

If you have been spending your money with one or more Directories, you must first determine your Return on Investment (ROI) before making any type of decision. (No matter what the innkeeper down the road told you about their favorite Directory!)

First, print out the traffic report your Directory sent you by e-mail. (If you deleted them, simply ask for an annual report and they will e-mail you a new one.) After you have the Directory report, print out the annual traffic report from your inn's server. (Your Webmaster can supply you with this report if you are unfamiliar with the control panel on your server.) If you are not interested in comparing the two documents, then elect to use the traffic report generated off your server – it will deliver you the most accurate statistics.

Now you are ready to calculate the cost of every visitor each directory sent to your inn's Web site. On the first directory report, find the total number of hits to your inn's Web site and divide this number into the annual cost of that directory. The result will be your cost-per-click or your cost-per-referred-visitor. Repeat this process for every directory you currently pay an annual fee.

ROI formula:

of hits * .01 = # of room nights booked
Multiply your room nights booked by your average rate

Did you cover your B&B Directory Investment? Which online B&B Directory listing has the best value for <u>your</u> inn?

Once you have calculated your ROI and paid your subscription fee, make sure you place a link on your inn's Web site back to all the directories you subscribe to, this will give your site the reciprocal link advantage (link popularity) that most search engines value.

Marketing will always be a gamble to some degree. When you win, your ROI is great. When you lose, your ROI is low. How do you decide how much to put into printed collateral, promotions, conferences, premiums, local events, Internet, and so much more?

Think of your marketing in terms of short term and long term returns. Some of your marketing efforts are intended to keep your local audience aware of your location and services.

On a broader basis you need to reach out to a more global market. To reach the global market at their point of sale decision, there is no better way than the Internet search engines.

Ask yourself a few questions about your Internet marketing and sales strategy. Do you have a pro-active search engine marketing program? Are your online sales producing your best ROI? Is the percentage of your investment budget comparable to your percentage of Internet business? For example, if 50% of your sales are originating online, is your Internet marketing budget 50% of your overall marketing budget?

Be sure to consider a percentage of your phone reservations when you analyze your Internet marketing results.

Your marketing decisions, of course, are affected by factors unique to your bed and breakfast such as location, local market conditions, room rates and seasonality. On the other hand, whatever these factors may be, in today's battle for market share, your sales are directly affected by the quality of your Web site and how your site is ranked on the major search engines.

Your final decision depends on how much of your overall room sales are coming from online sources. If you don't know what phone reservations are generated by your Web site you need to setup a special toll free number on your site. The rule of thumb used to expect innkeepers to average two phone bookings for every online booking, this is rapidly changing as more and more Americans turn to the Internet to plan and book their travel accommodations.

Real-time Internet Reservation Services

Over the past few years, the Internet has changed the way Americans book travel. As a society, we have become far more empowered and are able to weigh decisions based on a wide variety of information. Utilizing the most powerful search engines such as Yahoo!, Google, MSN and others, in combination with travel directories potential guests come to your Web site to view the most complete, most up to date information. To compete in this global marketplace of the 21st Century, every B&B Web site should have real-time Internet reservation services that can show visitors an availability calendar and allow them to book their accommodations.

There are a number of excellent real-time Internet reservation services out there, but Webervations.com is the only such service endorsed by the Iowa Bed & Breakfast Innkeeper's Association, and the company services some of the finest bed and breakfast properties in the nation.

One of their best features is called "Instant Online Availability." Any online changes you make to your availability schedule will be instantly reflected on your Web site's availability calendar, as well as any other Webervations.com related page.

The system also has a credit card validation feature in the reservation engine. This feature uses a mathematical formula to check credit card numbers for accuracy as they are entered into the booking form. It eliminates the chance of a guest making a mistake as they enter their billing information with their reservation or reservation request.

Many of today's national lodging directories will display your Webervations.com online availability on your directory listing. Here is a list of the lodging directories that currently display Webervations.com availability on listings:

* Bed and Breakfast Inns Online (www.bbonline.com)
* BnBFinder (www.bnbfinder.com)
* International Bed and Breakfast Pages (www.ibbp.com)
* ILoveInns.com (www.iloveinns.com)
* Bed & Breakfast Inns of N America (www.inntravels.com)
* Bed and Breakfast List (www.bnblist.com)
* The Innkeeper B&B Guide (www.theinnkeeper.com)
* Charming Country Inns (www.charmingcountryinns.com)
* BedandBreakfast.com (www.bedandbreakfast.com)
* Select Registry (www.selectregistry.com)
* Top 10 Inns (www.top10inns.com)
* Cabins and Resorts (www.cabinsandresorts.com)
* 1st Travelers Choice (www.virtualcities.com)

The Webervations.com system will allow your guests to submit requests for Gift Certificates. Like the Availability Calendar, this section is also tied to their secure server, which will allow you to collect your guest's credit card information. When you receive an order, all that you need to do is process the credit card, and then send the gift certificate to the address that was collected with the order.

Another feature of the Webervations.com system is the Inn Store section. It is best used for "Add-Ons" or "Concierge" items. This feature will allow you to display items to your guest that they would add on to their reservation.

And, if your computer skills are a bit lacking and you need some telephone assistance, you'll be pleased with their free technical support team. Webervations.com is known for outstanding customer service. The Supervisor of Technical Support, Willie Louthen-Brown, trains and manages a support team with an on-going goal of ensuring optimal productivity and quality customer satisfaction. The annual rates are affordable, there are add-on features, and the system works for any size property. Reach them at (740) 385-4444 or go directly to their Web site at: **www.webervations.com**.

Make Time for Internet Marketing, Especially Blogging

In the early days of the Web, just having a Web site listed in the major search engines brought traffic to most Web sites. And interesting content encouraged return visits. Today, more often than not, innkeepers can be disappointed in the number of visitors to their Web sites. Their disappointment has nothing to do with the design of their site or the quality of the services they offer. It has everything to do with competition.

With millions of pages already on the Web, and more posted online every day, getting your Web site noticed isn't easy. Innkeepers today must learn about Internet marketing.

Internet marketing is one of the hottest, but also one of the most misunderstood, topics of interest for the innkeeping community.

One exciting way to increase traffic and push Web site rankings up in search engines is the practice of blogging.

A few years ago few people had ever heard the word blog – now, you hear about them everywhere, from the beauty shop to the national television news stations.

Here is a quick run-down of why search engines have a love affair going with blogs:

- **Blogs are relevant, organized, and contain subject-specific content:** Search engines love relevant content that's organized in simple, intuitive fashion -- similar to site maps.
- **Blogs tend to index easily:** With a blog, the search engines can read the content much easier because there's nothing to get in the way. Few graphics, no Flash movies or complex javascript, just pure, well-organized text.
- **Frequently updated content:** New content is a signal to the search engines to visit more frequently. The more frequently they visit, the more they'll index, and the better your chances of getting higher rankings.
- **An abundance of links:** Blogs allow links and these links make a search engine's job a lot easier. Search engines generally index a site by following one link to another.

As a Web designer I love blogs because they give the client more control over their Web presence, which in turn creates a more satisfied customer. They also improve the Internet skills of clients. Once a blog is configured, it is an easy task for an innkeeper to go in and post. The more they post, the more they want to learn about the technology. It is a win-win situation for everyone concerned, from the innkeeper to the inn traveler to me, the Web site designer!

So, what is a "Blog"?

The word "Blog" is an abbreviated version of "weblog," which is a term used to describe web sites that maintain an ongoing chronicle of information. From a layperson's point of view it is a diary-type commentary that contains links to additional places on the Internet. Blogs can focus on a particular topic, such as Iowa travel, or they could be of a more personal nature – one author simply journaling about daily life and their thoughts.

We are going to focus on one specific blog application: **Wordpress**. At any time you can find additional instructions on Wordpress at their Web site: www.wordpress.org. We are also going to focus on how an innkeeper can use a Wordpress blog to market their B&B.

The content on a blog consists of articles (generally referred to as "posts" or "entries") that author(s) write. Blog authors can compose their articles in a web-based interface, built into the blogging system itself. This interface is accessed with an ID and a password. What Do Innkeepers blog about?

Here are a few posts taken off the IBBIA blog located at **http://iabedandbreakfast.com/blog**

Hampton Iowa Bed and Breakfast Winter Fun
January 21st, 2007

The snow has arrived and now is the time to have some winter fun at Country Heritage Bed and Breakfast Hampton Iowa. If you enjoy snowmobiling than our bed and breakfast is the place to be. The groomed snowmobile trail is right at our doorstep. We have ample room for snowmobile trailers so bring your friends and enjoy our luxurious accommodations while having a great time. What is better than riding the trails and than relaxing in front of the fireplace or in the whirlpool tub. Please join us for a great time. Make your reservation on line at http://www.countryheritagebb.com or call 866-456-4036.

Romantic Valentine's Lodging at Forest City, Iowa Bed & Breakfast

January 18th, 2007

My Special Valentine stay says "I love you" at the Elderberry Inn Bed and Breakfast in Forest City, Iowa. The Special Valentine stay is an opportunity to treat your sweetheart to a one-night stay in the Woodlands suite. The Woodlands Suite has a private double whirlpool, comfy robes and a fireplace to relax by. This offer also includes a bottle of sparkling juice, chocolates, evening dessert, and a three course breakfast. My Special Valentine package is $125. We would be happy to accept your reservations at 641-581-2012.

New IBBIA Inn located in Atlantic Iowa

January 14th, 2007

Harrisdale Homestead Bed & Breakfast
60182 Dallas Road, Atlantic, IA 50022
Phone (712) 243-3310 or (712) 254-2254

Harrisdale Homestead is a farmhouse set on a real working farm. It has simple accommodations in a rural setting. A welcoming 1920s farmhouse on a working century farm. Stay in one room, or reserve the whole house. Meals available. More information about the Homestead can be found at www.harrisdale.com

Elkader Opera House 2007 Schedule
Wednesday, January 3rd, 2007

Make plans to stay at Cedar St Suites! (A Two bedroom Suite with full bath, living room, kitchen, and sleeper sofa.) Check out the 2007 season at the historic Opera House in Elkader, next to our new suites. Sunday Matinee Piano Series begin January 28. The spring play is Noises Off in April. The Magic Lantern Show is February 12. Call Cedar Street Suites to check on availability at: Phone: 563-245-3221 or our Cell Phone at 563-880-1233 for outstanding lodging accommodations for all Opera House performances.

Timberpine Lodge Valentine Package
Tuesday, January 2nd, 2007

Valentine's Day will be here before we know it and your special someone would love a weekend or overnight in our cozy Timberpine Lodge. One night in our Pinecone Suite with candlelite dinner and roses in your room for $225.00 per night. Book early to take advantage of this offer. Visit us online at www.timberpinelodge.com

Our Tara Inn Representing IBBIA in Northeast Iowa
January 14th, 2007

Our Tara Inn 1231 Highway 9 Lansing, IA 52151
Phone (563) 568-2665 or (563) 380-8272
Sleeps 6 with one private bedroom and bath

Our Tara Inn features a panoramic view of three states: Iowa, Minnesota and Wisconsin. Look for deer, turkey and eagles that appear frequently in our area. Sportsmen can enjoy 1500 acres of state land nearby. Stocked trout streams include French Creek, Village Creek and Clear Creek. And don't forget to visit the mighty Mississippi River, only seven miles from Our Tara Inn. Come experience Iowa's own "Little Switzerland"! Visit www.ourtara.com

B&B of Cabin Cove Joins IBBIA
January 14th, 2007

Bed and Breakfast of Cabin Cove
820 Indiana Avenue Iowa Falls, IA 50126
Phone (641) 648-9571

At the Bed and Breakfast of Cabin Cove in Iowa Falls, Iowa, inn travelers will enjoy a peaceful rest in the log cabin or guests can step outside and discover the Butterfly house, or take a walk in the woods. They are open all year round. Check them out any season, and you'll find you especially enjoy the wonderful winter scenery on the Iowa River before it turns to spring. The central location in the state is a real plus. Visit the Web site at http://www.bbcabincove.com/ for more photos and details about the immediate area.

Storm Lake, Iowa, Luxury Bed and Breakfast
Saturday, January 6th, 2007

Metcalf House B&B now includes a full floor luxury four room Suite. The Suite is perfect for honeymooning and anniversary celebrations. We welcome any couple desiring a romantic getaway.

The Luxury Suite features a high quality queen-sized bed with a access to a private balcony a view of Storm Lake. The suite also offers a separate sitting room, a full bathroom with a double whirlpool tub. Enjoy your morning breakfast in your own private bistro setting.

Call ahead and make your appointment for a private massage in our new spa room. Rates start at $61.00 per night. Visit us on line at http://www.metcalfhouse.com

These are a few ideas that might help give you ideas for the blogging posts you'll want to place on your Web site's blog. You can find the ones above and a lot more online at: http://iabedandbreakfast.com/blog

The Wordpress blog software makes it possible for the most novice computer user to create posts and market their inn on the Internet.

Wordpress is public domain software. It is a bit challenging to install on a server, but there are hosting companies with technical support for this specific public domain software. Yet another reason to like it.

Wordpress has some very nice features that are fairly easy to master. But, you don't have to learn how to use them all in order get started. Learn and use the basics first and then slowly add other skills as you become more and more comfortable posting.

I consider the "write a post" and the "upload an image" functions to be the two most important ones to learn. Once you have these two skills, adding more will happen almost naturally.

Here is a list of a few features in the Wordpress software that innkeepers can utilize:

Post to the Future

Write a post today, have it appear on the weblog at a future date, automatically.

Multi-paged Posts

If your post is too long, cut it up into pages, so your readers don't have to scroll to the end of the world.

File/picture Uploading

You can upload pictures or files, and link to them or display them in your articles. You have the option of creating thumbnails of pictures when you upload them.

Save Drafts

Save your unfinished articles, improve them later, publish when you're done.

Previewing Posts

Before you press the "Publish" button, you can look at the preview for the article you just wrote to check if everything is the way you want it. In fact, you can do that at any time, since the preview is "live".

Searching

WordPress has a functional built-in search tool, which allows visitors to the blog to search for terms they are interested in.

Moderation

For the control freak in all of us, WordPress provides an array of moderation options. You can moderate:

- all comments before they appear on the blog
- comments with specific words in them
- comments posted from specific IP addresses
- comments containing more than some specified number of links.

All these moderation options keep spammers and vandals in check.

Notification

WordPress can keep you in the loop by sending you an e-mail each time there is a new comment or a comment awaiting moderation. You make the decision to keep or delete the comment.

Writing Your Blog Posts

Think in terms of keywords and keyword phrases. You can still embellish with hospitality terms like "breathtaking views" and "exceptional ambience," just be sure you include bed and breakfast keywords such as:

> Bed and Breakfast, b and b, country inn, romantic getaway, week-end getaway, lodging, BnB, accommodations, luxury accommodations, lodging, bed and breakfast, vacation, vacation, family vacation, intimate vacation, travel, travel lodging, lodging, bed and breakfast lodging, etc.

When writing blog posts keep the potential guest at the forefront of your mind. Write about travel tips, packing tips, driving tips and other topics inn travelers care about.

Do your best not to do a hard sell on your blog. Lodging packages are excellent for blog posts. They sell your inn, but in a manner that is highly desired by your reading public.

Here are a few more posting tips:
- Keep your posts relatively short. Write as if you were in a conversation with someone, after all one of the goals of the blog is to get readers engaged and leaving comments.

- Use photos sparingly. The search engine "spiders" can index the IBBIA blog (and Web site) in a more efficient manner if they encounter few photographs or graphics of any nature.

- Somewhere in your post, link to your personal Web site. A serious lodging prospect will go and visit your inn's Web site where they will find complete information on booking a stay at your establishment.

- Watch your spelling and language use. Use the build-in spell checker. If you are a poor typist, take a typing class! Make an effort to improve your skills. Like it or not, the computer is a tool every innkeeper should master.

- Don't put your e-mail address in your posts. You don't want to increase your exposure to e-mail spammers.

- If you enter a lodging special package, always include a price and an expiration date. The expiration date is critical because blogs are archived and you don't want a potential guest to find a two-year-old lodging special and hold you to the two-year-old price listed.

- Seldom post photographs, and only post photographs that tell a story. Photos slow down the indexing process of the search engine robots. Don't use an image unless it is an exceptional photo that can tell a story better than text on the page. And, make sure you compress and reduce all images to a .jpg file that is no larger than 300 pixels wide – for best results.

Finding Time for Internet Marketing

"As a busy innkeeper, I don't have time to do Internet marketing." It's a common complaint I hear regularly from Bed and Breakfast owners. When you are the only one who can serve the clients, manage the business, and perform all the sales and marketing functions, time becomes the most precious commodity you have. How can you find time for Internet marketing with so many other important priorities?

There are many time management techniques at your disposal. You can delegate tasks, chunk down projects to smaller steps, and set aside time on your calendar for making calls, writing blog posts, or updating marketing print materials. Then again, maybe you have already tried all those methods and discovered that time is still scarce.

Maybe the real answer is not to find more time for Internet marketing, but to MAKE time.

Every day, you take part in many time-consuming activities that don't include marketing, yet marketing is the one activity that will ensure your business new customers. And, with so many potential guests now using the Internet as their prime source of locating lodging accommodations for week-end, business, and vacation travel, how can justify not MAKING time to do Internet marketing?

Blog Posts Take Minutes to Create

The Wordpress blog is fairly user-friendly. Once you have learned how to create a post on your Wordpress blog, you are ready to schedule a daily time to create posts. Since it is best to keep your blog posts short, you won't need to block out more than 30 minutes a day to devote to creating blog posts.

In today's competitive hospitality Internet market, you must commit to making time for Internet marketing—whether you're posting daily on your blog, attending Internet marketing workshops, preparing to add the next page to your existing Web site, or creating an e-mail newsletter -- without a strong commitment, you'll find yourself consistently putting off your Internet marketing efforts.

Make the decision today, to devote time to Internet marketing, and reap its future rewards as you connect with new guests and expand your Internet marketing skills.

Notes:

Chapter Seven
Showcase Your Destination Online

Anyone can sit at a computer and write short blog posts urging inn travelers to visit his/her inn. But the innkeeper that can virtually help readers truly understand a destination can use destination blogging to connect with potential guests, promote his/her destination, and create a richer experience for visitors which ultimately results in increased customer loyalty.

Innkeepers live in the local area and know the destination in-depth. This sense of place enables them to infuse each blog post with an insider's perspective.   The end result of destination blogging is expansive and controlled.

An excellent example of "destination blogging" can be seen at: http://iabedandbreakfast.com/blog/?p=1027

The Web has a way of changing things as we know them. A daily journal of thoughts, observations and insight — posted on the Internet — can be a way to boost your business and bring new visitors to your destination.

Blogs are more than a passing Internet fancy, and they are a powerful Internet marketing tool. They have become a way to engage and inform readers and potential customers of businesses large and small. Blogging is a fantastic way to keep in touch with your guests and keep them informed about your property and your destination. Your blog can help visitors will find all the information they need on local shopping, restaurants, sights and attractions as well as local culture.

A significant amount of people stay at B&Bs because of local events, attractions, things to do, etc. Therefore, blogs showcasing local destinations can be a highly successful form of Internet marketing for any bed and breakfast inn.

Blogs are Considered Social Media

Social media is a collective term for online "technologies and practices that people use to share opinions, insights, experiences, and perspectives." (*Wikipedia*) The term started with Rohit Bhargava of Ogilvy Public Relations back in 2006.

Social media can take many different forms, including text, images, audio, and video. The social media sites typically use tools like message boards, forums, podcasts, bookmarks, communities, wikis, weblogs, etc. Social media includes social media applications like Wikipedia (reference), MySpace (social networking), Gather.com (social networking), YouTube (video sharing), Second Life (virtual reality), Digg (news sharing), Flickr (photo sharing) and Miniclip (game sharing).

Social media, or Internet media, has the ability to allow people to interact in some way. Many blogs are a two way street, inviting readers to post feedback on what they see. While other blogs may prefer to only allow its owners to post and not allow comments. (The ability to allow comments is always available, but the owner may elect to turn this option on or off at will.)

A Short Blog Glossary

In another step towards understanding blogs, it is important to get familiarized with some key terms used in the blog world. Most of these have already been explained in other chapters, but additional exposure to these words at this point seems appropriate.

- **Blogging** – The activity of updating a blog

- **Blogger** – Someone who writes/posts contextual content or photos in a blog

- **Blogosphere** - Community of bloggers

- **Posts** – A post is an article or a comment written on a blog

- **Trackback** – A method for Web authors to request notification when somebody links to one of their documents. Trackbacks enable authors to keep track of who they are linking to or referring to their articles

- **RSS** – Real Simple Syndication

- **Web Syndication** -Refers to making Web feeds available from a site in order to provide other people with a summary of the website's recently added content

- **Content Syndication** – Ability for others to subscribe to the content on your site (using RSS feeds)

- **Socializing the blog** – Promoting your blog by asking relevant bloggers to review your site by posting, commenting and linking

Notes:

Secrets to Making Your Lodging Blog Successful

Here's a little secret, *search engines crave content*. Okay so maybe it's not such a big secret, but if you go and review a number of lodging Web sites you'd begin to think it so. Unfortunately, too many Web sites just sit there doing nothing month after month – and in some cases, year after year.

Providing content, not to mention fresh content, is one of the toughest chores of anyone who maintains a Web site. But when it comes to generating traffic for the 21st Century Internet it is the most important job. Blogs, by their very nature, are all about content. In a commercial environment, every blog entry is fresh content. If you will make time to get in the habit of creating two, three, even four entries a week on your blog, you will soon have a content building bonanza on your hands.

Another advantage that blogs seem to currently possess over traditional web pages and sites is lack of competition. While the number of bloggers increases daily, there are still relatively few commercial lodging blog sites.

The very first bed and breakfast "inn traveler" blog in the nation was uploaded to the Iowa Bed and Breakfast Innkeepers Association server in February of 2006 at **http://iabedandbreakfast.com/blog**. It was introduced that year at their annual conference held in Iowa City by the association's executive board. Following closely in their footsteps was the Minnesota Bed and Breakfast Association with their blog found at http://minnesotabedandbreakfasts.org/nucleus/. Today there are a growing number of bed and breakfast "inn traveler" blogs found on the Internet. Some do an excellent job of portraying their destination as a mecca to the inn traveler, while many others are not kept up-to-date or are filled with sales pitch content that tends to waste the time of the visitor.

As a general rule, I am adamant that business bloggers should host their content on their own servers. Nobody — not Blogger, not our friends at WordPress, not MySpace — should have control over where or how your B&B content is hosted. A business blog running on your own domain, on your own servers, means that nobody controls your content but you. Facebook, a social networking system, holds a lot of promise, but it can't promise that you'll be in control of your content. Blogging is a medium with real staying power, but blogging is just one tool in the innkeeper's arsenal that needs to be mastered. The Internet is an ever-changing environment where it is important to have control over the business content you generate.

For those of us that have been blogging for some time, our blogs have also become archival footage in a way. I'm often referred back to posts I wrote six months ago or a year ago. One of the early examples of a major breaking news event for the bed and breakfast industry through a blog is when the Iowa Bed & Breakfast Innkeepers Association let me break the news that they were launching their blog officially at the conference. Someone wrote me recently and said, "Remember that post?" The Iowa B&B blog is no longer an experiment, but a working model for all other state associations.

5 Secrets to Successful Destination Blogging

Here are 5 Blogging Secrets for innkeepers desiring to maintain a successful blog presence on the Internet. The apply whether you are posting on an association blog or one sitting on the server that also contains your bed and breakfast site. (The most effective blogs are hosted on the same server you host your B&B Web site on. Using one of the free blogging options on the Internet will not serve you as well in the long run.)

1. Talk about your destination, local area attractions and exciting information, rather than always about your lodging property. Give the reader a sense of the area's culture. Try to explain the all about the community and

your society in terms of social norms and preferences. Talk about upcoming events, local food preferences, sights to see, and attractions to visit. Use photos to evoke a sense of place when necessary. Write in a casual tone, just as you would talk to a guest. Tell your own stories in your own words. If your B&B has an interesting history, write about it. If your B&B caters to families or people traveling with pets, write about it, or tell some funny stories about some of the kids or pets that have stayed at your inn. (Don't post real names or the city they come from without permission, and never post a photo of a guest or their pet without written permission.)

2. Commit time to manage your blog – unlike your Web site, your blog does require commitment of your time. Moderate your blog carefully on a weekly basis if you are going to allow visitors to comment on your posts. Socialize with bloggers who are blogging about your area and request that they review your blog.

3. Convert readers by offering time sensitive lodging offers, discount tickets to attractions, and information about local deals, dining, shopping, etc.

4. Offer the ability to make a reservation online from your blog.

5. Under a dining category, add posts about your favorite restaurants. Add a personal touch by offering great recipes from your chef -- post popular recipes, especially those your guests have requested.

Promoting Blogs

The task of blog and web site promotion is never ending. Good computer skills, however, make the undertaking much easier. If you are not very good at using your computer, it is time to go and enroll at a local community college and take a few classes. At the very minimum, you need to know how to use your specific e-mail program, how to effective use search engines, and how to resize digital photographs. (Typing with more than two fingers is also a worthwhile skill for the 21st Century!) Without basic computer skills, the job of Internet marketing will frustrate, anger and confuse you. So, if you need classes, don't procrastinate, just sign-up and go take them. You'll be glad you did.

Now, with basic computer skills, here are some steps you can take to promote your blog. The more action steps you will take, the more successful you will be and the more ROI you will gain.

- Enroll your blog in to blog search engines.

- Enroll your blog RSS in to RSS search engines.

- Tell guests about your blog and the flexibility of adding comments if you are going to elect to use the comment function in your blog. (You can always turn it off if the spammers begin to fill your comment posts with too much trash.) If you are going to allow comments on your blog posts, make sure to moderate your comments regularly. Blogs can add further leverage to the frequency with which search vehicles identify you and your company, particularly if your blog allows readers to post a response. Search engines tend to prefer bigger Web sites. With blogs that allow comments, every new post and every new comment becomes an additional Web page filled with additional keywords to be picked up by the search engine spiders.

- Offer time sensitive lodging offers, such as hot deals and special packages at least two to three times a month. Send an e-mail campaign to let people know that they can find offers only on your blog.

- Socialize your blog - this is a very important step towards promoting your blog. You have to seek out bloggers who are blogging about your area and your topics. It is easy to find bloggers specific to your industry by using blog search engines such as Technorati.com. Make a list of relevant bloggers and write about their blog on your blog. Ask these bloggers to review your blog. If they find your blog relevant and informational, they will post positive reviews on their blog about your blog and will give your blog a very qualitative link.

- If you are a member of a state B&B association, ask other members to review your blog and comment on it in their blog or on the association's blog. If they have stayed as a guest at your inn, ask them to tell about their experience on their blog.

- Inform and train your employees to be aware of the blog and be a part of the promotional strategy. When they answer a call, they should be able to provide additional information about the blog and the special lodging offers it contains.

- Blogging can also address other needs, some of which supersede a simple profit motive. For instance, as an innkeeper you can use your blog to vent your frustration about everything from the public's notions about "all B&Bs are geared for romance" to public misconceptions about health issues like bed bugs.

- Register with blog search engines – search engines that specialize in blogs. They include:
  http://www.daypop.com
  http://www.blogvision.com
  http://www.blogsearchengine.com

- Register with blog directories – online directories that specialize in blogs. They include:
  http://www.eatonweb.com ($15.00 per year fee to be included in this directory)
  http://www.zimbio.com (free directory plus article publishing tools)
  http://www. blogarama.com (excellent resource)

The Role of Patience in Successful Blogging

One way to get up to speed on what to say is to read other blogs and, in turn, offer your own viewpoint on any given topic for which you know something about. It's not a matter of competing with other blogs, because even if a nearby B&B has a blog, it won't be the same as yours. You have your own story to tell in your own voice. Be patient with yourself, but make a commitment to acquire outstanding blogging skills and use them to generate higher search engines rankings in a cost-effective manner that promotes your property and helps keep rooms filled for years to come.

Get into the practice of "blogrolling." Getting regular visitors to your site isn't just a matter of fresh, insightful commentary. Building traffic between blogs and Web sites is another central element to luring repeat visitors. Here, "blogrolling" is an effective tool. This, in essence, is a set of links on your blog site that identifies other sites on the Internet --- related to your B&B, the B&B industry or your guests --- which you find valuable. Developed in conjunction with a fresh voice, blogrolling encourages a steady back and forth between various sites, including other blogs. Write commentary about what other bloggers have written, then link to them. This tactic really gets you into the overall bloggers' pool.

During a guest's visit, get into the habit of discussing the Internet. Ask guests if they have a Web site and if they'd be interested in a link to their site from your blog. Often – if not always – they'll say yes and link back to your blog or Web site. A large collection of incoming links help raise your Internet profile and ranking at the various search engines.

Learn how to emphasize keywords in your blog posts. Search engine hits are another element of generating traffic. One strategy to attract search engine interest is through careful use of keywords in both your title headlines and blog copy. For instance, if a post topic focuses on the use of organically grown produce, use of the words "organic" and "produce" as often as possible and in varied permutations can help push your blog site toward the head of the search engine line. Stay on one topic per post, so your content is focused on keywords, and link to other blogs on this subject in your post.

Keep content fresh. One cardinal snafu that can bring down even the best intentioned of blogs is stale content. Nothing is more discouraging to prospective guests, or faithful guests, than returning to a blog site to find old or outdated material when they are seeking the latest news from your destination. So, be prepared to work at keeping your blog as fresh and current as possible. And, when you add a new category to your blog, be sure at least one of your static Web site pages contains a link to this new category. (Since your blog is also a Web site, your Webmaster can link to the various blog categories or even just one post. This type of cross-exchange of links on your server will, over time, generate more traffic and improving your search engine findability.)

It is important to not only keep fresh content on your blog, but also noteworthy content. That doesn't necessarily mean you need to create posts as lengthy as a Michener novel, because many engaging blogs are created with short, concise messages. But make a commitment to update your blog on as regular basis as your schedule reasonably permits.

Watch your traffic closely. Monitor the amount and quality of the traffic you receive. If things seem slow or stagnant, don't be gun-shy about varying your subjects to boost interest. (And, if you have a topic that is seldom accessed, then don't waste time with it any longer.) But don't stray too far from the B&B lodging topic or tourism in general.

Over time, begin to participate in the Blogosphere, the community of bloggers. BlogExplosion.com is a blogging community where people can find and read your blog, get your blog reviewed or even chat with other bloggers all around the world! If you are new to the Blogosphere, BlogExplosion.com is a good place to start a free account and begin talking with other bloggers, plus the site has a number of blogging tools that will help drive traffic to your blog. Whether you like to talk about your local events, your destination, or simply enjoy sharing your B&B life experiences on your blog with other people BlogExplosion.com is a great way to expand the number of people that read your blog!

LinkBaiting and Your Blog

Linkbaiting is the process by which you write an article or post that makes waves within your industry or state. To create a great linkbait you **start with something interesting, maybe something controversial, possibly something well researched, or something very unique**. Then take this piece of information or article, put a great headline on it, and let your readers submit it to Digg, Del.icio.us, and other social media sites. This process will get your blog post buzzing around the Blogosphere very quickly.

There is one crucial key to linkbaiting. **Don't recycle or copy content!** If you must use someone's text, be sure you give him/her credit somewhere in the post. It is best, however, to use unique, great content, even if it takes a week to write one piece!

What is Link Bait?

Link bait is any content or feature within a website that somehow baits viewers to place links to it from other websites (*Wikipedia*).

A link to your site is a vote for your site. In reality the term 'link baiting' is a new term for something that Webmasters have been doing for many years.

There is a great deal of debate around both the term 'link baiting' and some of the practices that people talk about it incorporating. Some argue strongly, including myself, that it is just a by-product of quality content. Others argue that many link bait strategies border on spam while others seem to talk about link bait as being the answer to all Web promotional problems. (More and more Search Engine Optimization firms are offering link baiting services.)

Like almost anything Internet, people can use link baiting strategies for good promotional purposes but also for spamming and dubious other wasteful practices.

"Link bait creation falls under the task of link building, and aims to increase the quantity of high-quality, relevant links to a website. Part of successful linkbaiting is devising a mini-PR campaign around the release of a link bait article so that bloggers and social media users are made aware and can help promote the piece in tandem. Social media traffic can generate a substantial amount of links to a single web page. Sustainable link bait is rooted in quality content." (*Wikipedia*)

RSS Feeds

Blogging would not be as valuable if an individual had to depend on the traditional methods for getting traffic to a Web site. But a new piece of technology gives you the capability of reaching tens of thousands of readers with the click of a button. This technology is called RSS — Real Simple Syndication. It is a means by which the content on your blog can be translated and distributed to thousands of users who have access to a "News Feed." For now this service can be found for no charge on the Internet, but like all other Internet services, this is subject to future change.

News feeds allow you to see when websites have added new content. You can get the latest headlines in one place, as soon as it's published, without having to visit the websites you have taken the feed from. Different news readers work on different operating systems, so you will need to choose one that will work with your computer. Many innkeepers prefer using the ones offered for free by Google and Yahoo!.

News Aggregators

Perhaps one of the most exciting features to come arrive on the Internet is the ability to make a distinction between news and spam — it is called the news aggregator. News Aggregators are software applications that poll the world of blogs at user-defined intervals and update themselves whenever they see something new. With a news aggregator, you choose the sources you'd like to read, and the software will poll those sources hourly, daily, weekly — as you've specified — and it will notify you when one of them changes.

Many companies are currently providing services to give you access to news feeds. They fall into two categories:

Web-based News Aggregators: Two of the popular aggregators on the Web are Bloglines (http://www.bloglines.com), and Blo.gs. (http://www.blo.gs). Simply register with either or both services--at no charge--then browse their database of blogs, and click the "subscribe" link for any that interest you. They'll be added to your personal space on the Web site, and you can make a bookmark to view them at your leisure.

Desktop News Aggregators: If you'd like to have news delivered directly to your desktop, you can download a news reader like Sharp Reader (http://www.sharpreader.net) or Feed Demon (http://www.bradsoft.com/feeddemon/). Like their Web-based counterparts, these two products enable you to specify which blogs (or news sources) you'd like to follow, and they will update them when they sense any changes. There is no charge for Sharp Reader. Feed Demon costs $29.95.

And, if you'd prefer to get your updates via e-mail, News Gator (http://www.newsgator.com/) can integrate itself with e-mail software including Microsoft Outlook®Express, Eudora, Entourage, others. Most innkeepers will find the newsgator.com free browser services will accommodate most of their news reading needs.

Thanks to the news aggregators, blogs are available to a staggering number of potential readers. As a blog owner, your task--at least initially--is to see to it that your current and potential guests have news aggregators, and that they have your blog listed in them. This task should be considered an "advanced blog user" task. It is best to learn to walk before you attempt to run!

As a news aggregator reader, your guests will be pleased to see that you keep your blog updated. You can be confidence that they're going to read what you've written, because they voluntarily subscribed to your news feed.

Once you've attracted a following, people will begin to seek out your blog for expert inn traveler advice and commentary on your destination and the happenings at your property. Your blog will become the go-to source for timely information about your area.

A Helpful Service Called Ping-O-Matic

Ping-O-Matic (http://www.pingomatic.com) is a free service that "pings" or notifies the most important news aggregators on the web that you've updated your blog. Now, you have the potential of being noticed by over 500,000 people. And not one of them will even consider the possibility that you're sending spam.

Most blogging software is automatically configured to ping at least one or two of the major search engines or news aggregators. If you have a Web design firm customize your blog, they can configure your blog to ping both news aggregators and search engines each time a post is submitted. If you are not sure about the ping capabilities of your blog, you can use the pingomatic.com services.

A blog will never replace e-mail—on a purely personal level – or a professionally designed Web site. But a blog is a perfect compliment to a Web site, and it will help you to reach a larger audience than you thought possible. And remember, each and every one of these potential guests are interested in hearing what you have to say about your destination and your operation.

Notes:

Chapter Eight
Emerging Hospitality Trend: Podcasting

A fairly new technology that is becoming popular in the hospitality industry is podcasting. Podcasting is a new way to distribute audio and video programming via the Internet. The term podcasting derives its name from Apple's iPod, but to create a podcast or even to listen to one, you don't need to own an iPod, or any portable music player for that matter. Software for downloading podcasts is available online, along with software for creating podcasts. The majority of podcasts are audio, but video podcasts are becoming more and more popular as the trend picks up momentum. Podcasting lets you create your own syndicated online talk show or radio program, with content of your choosing.

Podcasts can contain information on attractions, activities in your area, local events, restaurant reviews, and any other data you might want travelers to know about your destination. These podcasts can be made available for download from the Web site of your Inn. They can be played immediately by destination-researchers on their computers, and/or be copied to an iPod or other portable digital-media player, to be brought along and listened to at the destination or while traveling to the destination. Like radio broadcasts, audio podcasts can be listened to while driving down the road.

A good example of an online traveler's podcast is on Frommers.com . Frommers has publish ed travel guidebooks for more than fifty years and now caters to online customers as well. You can find a link to the Frommers podcast page on their home page . There, you can find link s to their "Arthur's blog , " "podcasts," and "deals and news." When you arrive on the Frommers.com podcast page, you'll find a "subscribe to feed" section at the top of the page. You'll also see how Frommers.com makes it easy for travel researchers to find their podcast page, because below each download text link is a brief description of the content of the podcast.

How Do Inn Travelers Find Sites Containing Podcasts?

As mentioned in previous chapters, consumers go online and use the top three search engines (Google, Yahoo! and MSN Live Search) to research and find travel sites. Generally, travel-researchers are going to choose a destination, or an itinerary of destinations, before beginning to seek out accommodations. If your Web site contains destination related materials, which it should, even if limited, the keyword phrases you use should show-up in destination searches and create an opportunity for the traveler to shop for destination and lodging at the same time.

If you take the plunge and add a page with podcasts to your Web site, be sure to use a descriptive title for the link to the actual podcast. It is also a good idea to give a brief description of the podcast. A paragraph or two is all that is necessary. The content in a podcast file cannot be read by the search engines, so having text on the page describing the content of each podcast becomes necessary if the search engines are to easily index the pages containing travel related podcasts.

Who is Listening to Podcasts?

As you might have suspected, as of this writing the podcast users of today are young, but recent research by Nielsen/NetRatings found the average age of podcast users to be increasing. Keep in mind, the young of today are the travel consumers of tomorrow.

How to Get Started Podcasting Today

Anyone with a computer and a computer microphone can produce a podcast using free or inexpensive software and some simple recording hardware . You can also hire a professional to produce podcasts from the materials you furnish. Either way, there are a number of good books on the market to help get you started .

- Podcasting: Do It Yourself Guide by Todd Cochrane (Wiley, 2005)

- Secrets of Podcasting by Bart G. Farkas (Peachpit, 2006)

- What No One Ever Tells You About Blogging and Podcasting: Real-Life Advice from 101 People Who Successfully Leverage the Power of the Blogosphere by Ted Demopoulos (Kaplan Business, 2006)

Technology and the B&B Owner

Every operator of a B&B, no matter how small, needs to keep an eye on what online marketing tools the 5 Star luxury lodging properties are using. They set the future standard of what travelers will grow to expect from the mid-range and economy lodging markets .

Providing your guests with the entertainment and business technology they desire is becoming a must in the 21st Century. Look how quickly it became a necessity to furnish guests with Wireless High Speed Internet Access.

The innkeeper of today must simply be forward thinking about upgrading guest facilities. Not frightened and worried about costs. With the proliferation of mobile devices such as personal digital assistants (PDAs), portable DVD players, MP3 players, and Smartphone devices, guests often arrive at the B&B with all the technology they need. Your challenge is to constantly keep finding a way to integrate these devices with existing inn amenities to create a better guest experience.

Why? Because the traveling public has the expectation that any quality lodging establishment will provide for more comfort and convenience than they have at home.

Jeanna M. Stavas spent 15 years in a high technology corporate career, but then one day decided she was ready to try something new and make a change. Wanting to return to the Midwest and to her roots, she became interested in purchasing a B&B and becoming a business owner/operator/innkeeper. She sought a profession where she could use her passions for cooking and people and take from her business skills and knowledge as well as my travel experiences and put them into a business: With a goal focused on a complete lifestyle change, she joined the IBBIA as an Aspiring Innkeeper and began her search. Her quest for just the right property took her on many excursions around Iowa, but she found her dream property in the nearby state of Nebraska.

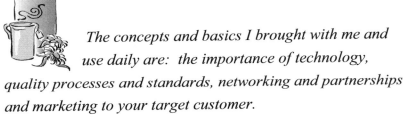

The concepts and basics I brought with me and use daily are: the importance of technology, quality processes and standards, networking and partnerships and marketing to your target customer.

I understand the importance technology has on the industry, both in having not only a web presence, but accepting online reservations and catering to your guests by offering wireless Internet access as well. As a single innkeeper, it's important to look for efficiencies and ways to save yourself time - my Web site offers photos, descriptions and an availability calendar so the potential guest has all the information they need right at their finger tips.

Also, you must implement and document standards, for operations and employees as well as for the quality you want to offer your guests, just as you would in any other business.

When I relocated and purchased my B&B in a small rural town, I had to "fit it". My first few months, I was out on the streets meeting with the other businesses in town, networking and partnering where I could. Two years later, I have learned who my guests are and have created packages and a lodging experience where they enjoy the unexpected extras and want for nothing but to stay longer!

Jeanna M. Stavas, Innkeeper
Whispering Pines Bed and Breakfast
21st Street and 6th Avenue
Nebraska City, NE 68410
(402) 873-5850/(877) 277-3577
www.bbwhisperingpines.com

You Have a Choice

Must every B&B adjust to all the trendy technology? Absolutely not. There remains many successful B&Bs across the nation that have no in-room phones, televisions or radios – these establishments usually market themselves as either "peaceful getaways" or "romantic getaways." So, without a doubt, it is possible to operate a successful B&B using the traditional means of recording keeping in a hand-written ledger, without a computer, printer or fax machine, and without any type of Internet access for guests.

However, the B&B that caters to the average inn traveler and to families had better stay aware of all the emerging trends and how they can boost the bottom line by putting-more-heads-in-the-beds. Increasing broadband usage by consumers, the preference to book lodging online, and the proliferation of techno gadgets will continue to change the Bed and Breakfast Industry. The savvy innkeeper will keep up with these changes, upgrade where necessary, and watch their business succeed as a result.

Stay on the Learning Curve!

Because today's technology changes so rapidly it will be critical to your long term success as an innkeeper to stay engaged in learning all you can about the Internet and all its various marketing opportunities.

As an Internet professional I am constantly reading and learning about new technologies as they emerge. You will want to do the same, but maybe at a little slower pace. Sign-up for automatic email newsletters from Internet professionals, let them do the research – you read about it.

Attend as many bed and breakfast conferences, workshop and seminars as you possibly can. This will keep you up-to-date on the latest lodging trends and keep you tapped into the innkeeping community.

And, don't think you have to just stay in your own state to attend conferences. Actively seek out educational opportunities that sound appealing to you. Maybe there is a speaker holding a workshop in a neighboring state that scheduled to give a demonstration on a topic that would highly benefit your inn, sign-up and get out there and network. You'll enjoy the break and meet some new innkeepers. And, whenever possible plan to stay at a B&B. Nila Haug, owner of the Golden Haug in Iowa City, Iowa, says, "an innkeeper can never visit too many inns! There is always something new to learn from the experience."

My husband and I love to travel and we make it a point to locate as many interesting and unique inns as possible on each and every trip we take these days. It's as if "the more inns we visit, the more inns we can't wait to visit!"

At quality B&Bs, we find that customers are truly guests, and it shows. There is almost always a snack waiting for us in our room, and the top-notch inns will have a small gift or flowers in the room. Most have private whirlpool tubs in the room, exceptionally good mattresses, plenty of towels, and white robes for use during our stay. Innkeepers gladly help us find the best restaurant in town, direct us to the most beautiful gardens in the nearby park, and much more.

If you come across an exceptionally unique inn during your travels, please log on to my Inn Traveler Blog at **http://totalwebdesigner.com/blog** and tell my readers all about it. Dedicated inn travelers love to hear about the unique or exceptional B&B experiences.

I hope you've learned a great deal from this publication and picked-up a multitude of useful hints and tips. Keep it on your desk near the computer for easy reference as you join other innkeepers in this most exciting industry!.

Before we started our B&B, we'd stay at a bed and breakfast inn and found the owners willing to share their wisdom with us. A B&B conference is that learning experience multiplied a thousand times by the value of the experts who speak at the conference, to the "everyday" experts running their own B&B's and sharing what they find works and doesn't in their business.

Virginia and Gary Walker
McNeill Stone Mansion B&B
1282 C Ave E
Oskaloosa IA 52577
641-673-4348
www.thestonemansion.com

Innkeeper Resources

Associations

Iowa Bed & Breakfast Innkeepers Association
P.O. Box 171
Spencer, IA 51301
800-888-4667 (inside Iowa) or 712-580-4242
Web site: www.iabedandbreakfast.com

This association offers educational Innkeeping Boot Camps based on the material in this book, and Aspiring Innkeepers receive a copy of this book with their membership packet.

Professional Association of Innkeepers International (PAII)
Web site: www.paii.org
E-mail: membership@paii.org
Headquarters: 207 White Horse Pike, Haddon Heights, NJ 08035
800.468.PAII (7244) or 856.310.1102

PAII often publishes industry statistics online, and they also have detailed industry research available for sale. Aspiring Innkeepers can contact request a free copy of their publication "Introduction to Innkeeping" – it is sent out by e-mail and postal mail.

Business Plan Consultants
 Inngenium LLC
 27 Elm Street
 Fryeburg, ME 04037
 (207) 221-5635
 Web site: www.inngenium.com

Graphic Design
 Graphic Details
 Contact: Angie Roberts
 Web site: www.gdetails.com

 Graphic Details is a design firm specializing in graphic
 design and print media. TotalWebDesigner.com is
 strategically partnered with Graphic Details to serve the Bed
 and Breakfast Innkeepers of America. Graphic design
 services for advertising, branding, logos, brochures and
 more is offered. The client list is impressive from AT&T to
 Universal Studios to Toyota, along with a growing number
 of bed and breakfast inns.

 TotalWebDesigner.com
 Custom Web Graphics for Hospitality Businesses
 Contact: Emily G. Boetel
 712.260.5372
 Web site: www.totalwebdesigner.com

Inn Brokers and Consultants
The B&B Team, Inc.
P.O. Box 399
Scottsville, VA 24590
Call 434-286-4600
Web site: www.bbteam.com

The B&B Team, Inc.
35 Western Ave., Suite 5
Kennebunk, ME 04043
Call 207-967-1995
Web site: www.bbteam.com

Innsitter
Harvest Moon Innkeeping
Interim Innkeeping for B&B Owners
Michelle Bliss - Interim Innkeeper trained by PAII
700 5th Ave SW • Altoona IA 50009
515.967.4103 or 515.689.8915
E-mail: michellebliss55@hotmail.com
www.harvestmooninnkeeping.com

Michelle's motto is "Caring for Your Business Your Way"
and she is available in all 50 states. Since she lives in Iowa,
most of her past assignments have been in Illinois and Iowa,
but she is well-prepared, and well-trained, to travel
anywhere in the USA for "innsitting" assignments. Michelle
has professional credentials and experience. Member of:
PAII, IIN (Interim Innkeepers Network), and two state B&B
associations – one of which is IBBIA.

Insurance

Tricor Hospitality Insurance Program
500 Iowa Street, Dubuque IA 52004
Contact: Chuck Andracchio
e-mail: candracchio@tricorinsurance.com
Toll Free: 800-556-5441 extension 1444

Licensed in Iowa, Illinois, Wisconsin, Minnesota, Missouri, and Nebraska. We can provide insurance tailored to fit your specific inn with features and endorsements for the innkeeper, guests and property of guests. However we can also provide important safety consulting since we have 3 safety engineers on our staff. We have also collected important links providing innkeepers with resources like architectural salvage, mortgage, clay/tile/metal roofs and many other areas of concern for innkeepers. We are members of local, state, regional and national innkeeper organizations so we stay in communication with experts in the industry. TRICOR is constantly searching the market for products specific to innkeeper protection.

James W. Wolf Insurance
PO Box 510, Ellicott City, MD 21041
Phone: 800-488-1135   Contact: James W. Wolf

"James Wolf Insurance is the largest provider of Innkeepers' Insurance in the United States. This was no accident. We took the time to learn the business, then designed an innovative insurance program to offer the most complete coverage for the inn, the owner, and the guest."

Heather White
Product Management Associate
Markel Insurance Company
804-965-1724 or Toll Free: 800-431-1270, ext. 1724
www.inninsurance.com

Markel Insurance Company—B&B Program offers specialized insurance protection to keep your B&B or country inn running smoothly. We offer general and umbrella liability, personal liability, fine arts, auto, employee dishonesty, and historic/unique property coverage. We also cover special events like weddings and special property like swimming pools.

Magazines

Bed & Breakfast America
Publisher/Innkeeper Advertising/Subscriptions
Phone: 580-529-3270
(*Between the hours of 8 a.m. - 5 p.m. CST*)
Web site: www.bba.travel

The B&B and Country Inn MarketPlace
Published 2x a year, features B&Bs for sale nationwide
926 Lenoir Rhyne Blvd., SE
Hickory, NC 28602
Email us at innsales@charter.net
Toll free 877-828-2323, Office: 828-324-7291

The Iowan Magazine
A Pioneer Communications Publication
218 6th Avenue
Suite 610
Des Moines, Iowa 50309
PHONE: 515.246.0402
FAX: 515.282.0125
Web site: www.iowan.com

Online B&B Directories

BEDANDBREAKFAST.COM®

700 BRAZOS STREET, SUITE B-700, AUSTIN, TX 78701
PHONE: 1-512-322-2710
FAX: 1-512-320-0883
SALES: 1-800-GO-BANDB (1-800-462-2632)

BBonline.com Bed and Breakfast Inns ONLINE
909 North Sepulveda Boulevard
El Segundo, CA 90245
toll free: (800) 215-7365 or (310) 280-4000
Web site: www.bbonline.com

Online Reservation Services

American Dreams Inc. - Webervations.com
Contact: Willie Louthen-Brown
84 E. Main St.
Logan, Ohio 43138
PHONE: 740-385-4444
FAX: 740-385-1625
Web site: www.webervations.com
E-mail: info@webervations.com

Webervations.com provides affordable, effective and
flexible online availability and reservation services to the
lodging industry. Webervations commitment to providing an
outstanding value means innkeepers only pay $80 per year.
There are no commission charges and there are no booking
fees.

Soap Amenities
> **Greenwich Bay**
> 5809 Triangle Dr.
> Raleigh, NC.27617
> Call Toll Free: 800-323-1209
> Web site: www.gbsoaps.com/contact.htm
>
> GREENWICH BAY is a family owned and operated business that has been manufacturing fine toiletries since 1962. All products are made to order using only the finest natural ingredients. We formulate, manufacture, design, print, package and ship from one location with skilled and experienced personnel. Your property logo and artwork are attractively displayed on all items.

Tax and Financial Services
> **Heying Tax & Financial Services**
> Contact: Alana Heying
> 714 South Grand Avenue, Suite B
> Spencer, IA 51301
> Phone: 712-580-3202
> Fax: 712-580-3203
> Web site: www.heyingtaxservices.com
>
> Tax, accounting, and consulting services to Bed & Breakfast owners and management. Allow them to focus on the tax and accounting aspects of your business so you can focus on your guests.

Web Design
> **TotalWebDesigner.com**
> PO Box D
> Fostoria, IA 51340
> Call 712-260-5372
> e-mail: Amelia@TotalWebDesigner.com
> **Web site: www.TotalWebDesigner.com**

Complete services for innkeepers from site development, to hosting, to monthly maintenance programs for Bed & Breakfast Associations. Rates are reasonable and customer services are superior. We also have a professional photographer on staff specializing in hospitality.

Web Design Client List includes: William Sauntry Mansion B&B, Timberpine Lodge, Water Street Inn, Loghouse & Homestead on Spirit Lake, Garden & Galley, Camp Bean Bed and Breakfast, The Stauer House Bed & Breakfast, Hannah Marie Country Inn, Serenity Bed and Breakfast, Iowa Bed & Breakfast Innkeepers Association, Minnesota Bed & Breakfasts Association, Nebraska Bed and Breakfast Association, Lake Country Bed & Breakfast Association, Okoboji Country Inn, the City of West Okoboji, and many more.

Graphic Details
Contact: Angie Roberts
Web site: www.gdetails.com

The client list is impressive from AT&T to Universal Studios to Toyota, along with a growing number of bed and breakfast inns.

Index

Link bait creation, - *182* -
link popularity, - *137* -
Linkbaiting, - *181* -
Local Media E-mail List, - 83 -
lodging directories, - *142* -
logo, - *57* -, - *58* -, - *59* -, - *71* -
Louthen-Brown, Willie, - *149* -, - *204* -
loyalty programs, - *45* -

M

Marilyn Meyer, *ii*
marketing materials, - *47* -, - *52* -, - *53* -, - *58* -, - *59* -, - *71* -
marketing voice, - *56* -
McNeill Stone Mansion B&B, - *198* -
media list, - *83* -
Metcalf House, - *6* -, - *24* -, - *156* -
Minnesota Bed and Breakfast Association, - *171* -
Muilenburg, Donna, - *103* -

N

nameservers, - *91* -
national lodging directories, - *142* -
negative cash flow, - *28* -
Network Solutions, - *91* -
news aggregator, - *184* -
news readers, - *183* -
Nichols, Mary, - *40* -, - *54* -
Norton, Liz, - *34* -, - *87* -

O

Occupancy and Revenue Forecasting, - *27* -
occupancy rates, - *19* -, - *29* -
Ogilvy Public Relations, - *166* -

Okoboji Country Inn, - *103* -
online distribution fees, - *74* -
online media distribution company, - *76* -
Open Directory Project, - *114* -
Our Tara Inn, - *155* -

P

PAII, - *41* -, - *71* -, -*199* -, - *201* -
PAII conferences, - *71* -
Personal Assessment Survey, - *3* -
Phillips, Jerry, - *5* -
photographs, - *66* -, - *68* -, - *69* -, - *70* -, - *77* -, - *79* -, - *81* -, - *110* -, - *161* -, - *174* -
Ping-O-Matic, - *186* -
podcasting, - *189* -
PR distribution, - *81* -
press release, -*73* -,
professional image, - *25* -
PRWeb, - *81* -

R

Reading from computer screens, - *79* -
Real Simple Syndication: RSS, - *183* -
real-time Internet reservation services, - *147* -
Roberts, Angie, - *59* -, - *200* --
room rates, - *8* -, - *19* -, - *37* -, - *39* -, - *40* -, - *146* -
room tax collection, - *17* -
RSS Feeds, - *183* -

S

search engine, - *75* -, - *92* -, -*109*-
search engine key terms, - *110* -

Made in the USA